THE SPIRIT OF GETTING ORGANIZED

The Spirit of

Getting Organized

12 Skills to Find Meaning and Power
in Your Stuff

PAMELA KRISTAN

Red Wheel
Boston, MA / York Beach, ME

First published in 2003 by
Red Wheel/Weiser, LLC
York Beach, ME
With offices at:
368 Congress Street
Boston, MA 02210
www.redwheelweiser.com

The quote on page 4 from Heather McHugh's unpublished
poem is used with her permission.

Library of Congress Cataloging-in-Publication Data
Kristan, Pamela.
  The spirit of getting organized : 12 skills to find meaning and power
in your stuff / Pamela Kristan.
      p. cm.
Includes bibliographical references and index.
    ISBN 1-59003-024-9 (PB)
1. Home economics. I. Title.
 TX147 .K65 2002
  640—dc21

                          2002151580

Typeset in Monotype Garamond by Gopa & Ted2

Printed in Canada

TCP

10 09 08 07 06 05 04 03
  8   7   6   5   4   3   2   1

Contents

Acknowledgments

As a SPIRITUALLY ORIENTED PERSON and an organization consultant, I've seen how organizing work touches every aspect of life, including the inner (and outer) reaches of philosophical inquiry and the social milieu in which we live. In this book I make such connections explicit. However, I am not by trade a philosopher or a social commentator, and, realize that at times I'm in deep water here. I send you, then, to the work of those who swim in these waters professionally. References to books by those who have influenced me appear in the Resources section.

Intellectual Debts

Jacob Needleman's books *Money and the Meaning of Life* and *Time and the Soul* give form to concepts that had been brewing in me for years. My thanks to him, also for leading me to Lewis Hyde's *The Gift* and Maurice Nicol's *Living Time*. Thomas Moore's books, *Care of the Soul* and *The Re enchantment of Everyday Life*, gave me similar gifts.

Many other authors influence my worldview in ways that show up here. David Abram and Brian Swimme both hitch paradigm-shifting ways of thinking to simple, intuitive concepts. In *The Spell of the Sensuous*, Abram uses metaphors of the past, present, and future to explain language; in *The Universe Is a Green Dragon*, Swimme uses metaphors of the four elements and sky to explain physical law. Susun Weed's wise woman way of fostering what is healthy rather than cutting away what is sick confirms the *both/and* principle that shows up in this book. Among other outside-the-box authors whose influence appears here are Daniel Quinn, Parker Palmer, and Karla McLaren. Thanks to all, and to the many others whose ways of thinking have contributed over the years.

Gratitude to Those Who've Helped Along the Way

I would like here to express my heartfelt and continuing gratitude to all those who helped, in ways obvious and not so obvious, to bring this work to life. All my clients and class participants: without you this book would not have been written. The book support team: Colleen Sharka, reader and support from the very beginning to the very end; Jim Guinness, always helpful with practicalities, not to mention way-out ideas; Glenn Morrow, expert, sensitive editor; Francine Crystal, tell-it-like-it-is-yet-gently reader; Carolyn Roosevelt, who knows all the right words; brainstorm session folks—Colleen, Jim, Francine, and Powell Woodward, Maria Judge, Rosemary Weiss, and Barbara Simkowski.

Those in my life who have cared for me when I needed it most: my sister Susan Olvey, Anne Marie Skogsbakken, Marlene Sinkuler, Medora Hearn, Barbara and Bonnie of Phoenix, without whose matter-of-fact, womanly care I might not be here. The Washington County folks who initiated me in Life/Death/Life: first and most deeply influential, Philip Batstone, from whom I learned how to sniff out structure in the surface; artist friends Elizabeth Ostrander and Vicky Southwell; Charlie Brown now gone; and Peter Milford, my muse all these years. Friends with whom I have shared intimately: Jane Hudson; Janet Piggins, who helped midwife my consulting business name, The Practical Matters; Jane Gallagher; Colleen; Jim; Anne Marie; and Christine Watson among them. And deep gratitude to the land that brings me forth and sustains me, especially fields and forests, swamps and rivers, and all the borders between.

Those who have profoundly influenced my spiritual life: Slow Turtle and Tlakaelel (thanks to Pat Connolly for bringing me to them); Paul Rezendes for introducing me to the art of seeing; Ross Jennings and the dowsers; and all the earth-spirituality folks encountered along the way.

Teachers, consultants, and madmen/women who have encouraged, shaped, and challenged me: Michael Steinberg, who brought me out as a writer; Life/Work Direction folks, Eunice & Don Schatz and Dick Faxon; Dan Cherry, who shakes me up homeopathically; Terri Fedrow, Lisa Caselli, Susan Pressman, Mark Weber, Ted Powers, Priscilla Mueller, Margo Mariana, Kurt Leland, Brother Blue, Phil, George Wertke, Walter Gray, and most especially, Tait Sanford Barrows.

Profound thanks—to all of you, and to the universe for bringing us together!

Prelude
Meaning and Power in Stuff

WHEN I FIRST STARTED WORKING in personal organization skills, it certainly didn't seem like I was doing anything deeply meaningful or earthshaking. Organizing was just something I could do that people needed. After years in the field, it slowly dawned on me that what I was doing was much more important than I realized. Is getting organized simply a matter of sorting papers, using file folders, and managing time? On one level, it is. And it's so much more.

Organizing can touch the whole of our being—not only the down-to-earth personal papers, files, and closets, but also the farthest-reaching, grand patterns of Nature. The papers on our desks are connected to the universe, and in fact, *are* the universe, in part. When we work with them, we work with the cosmos. What happens in the small influences what happens in the large. Getting organized is much more than scut work; it is an encounter with meaning and power.

Organizing also operates on a most intimate, personal level. When we organize soulfully, our particular way of being is reflected in our environment. How we think, how we do what we do, and how we envision ourselves come forward into the world. For example, when we throw things out, we're confronted with the values that tell us what to keep and what to toss. When we rearrange space, we put our stamp on our surroundings so we can effectively engage with the world as we choose. Through organizing we can get to know ourselves in all our fullness.

Organizing calls on our most human talents—perceiving patterns and participating in how those patterns play out. As we sort, we perceive the patterns that give our stuff sense and meaning. As we make changes, we participate in shaping our environment so our power can flow. By exercising these particularly human talents we enliven our souls and take our places as co-creators in the world.

I. Knowing Versus Doing

FOR MOST OF US, organizing seems to be mere drudgery—distasteful, trivial business when compared to the creative, productive, or urgent pursuits we feel called to do. If we see this as an *either/or* situation—either drudgery or productivity—guess which wins out? The important pursuits of our daily lives, not the trivial pursuit of organizing. Yet, when we pursue only productivity, we have nagging anxieties about organizing; when we pursue only organizing, we feel we're missing out on life.

Changing our perspective from *either/or* to *both/and* shows organizing as a valid pursuit in itself. Organizing supports and upholds us. It gets our down-and-dirty systems in place so we can reach the heights and explore the depths. Organizing is a not a primary goal; it is, in fact, secondary. Nonetheless, it requires appropriate attention. Without such attention, organizing can suck up all of our energy, throw a veil of cobwebs over our life, and muscle its way into the driver's seat to tell us where to go. However, if we pay proper *both/and* attention to organizing, it is perfectly willing to take the back seat.

We might think we're putting organizing in its place when we hold our nose, close our eyes, and do it as mindlessly as possible. But what are the consequences of dismissing a necessary part of life? Diminishing any part of our self diminishes our whole self. When we pull back energy from our stuff, we become constricted, inflexible, and shut down. When we operate mindlessly, that's exactly what we become—mindless. Life holds less and less meaning for us, becoming the Hell that Jacob Needleman talks about in his book *Money and the Meaning of Life*—the place of ever-diminishing being.[1] If we shun our stuff, we shun our rich, complex life; if we embrace our stuff, we embrace our wholeness.

FROM KNOWING TO DOING

With the prospect of getting organized before us, we can get profoundly discouraged. How often have we lamented, "I *know* what to do, I just don't *do* it!" The gap between knowing and doing can be a yawning chasm. A line from an early poem by Heather McHugh reads, "Nothing stands in my way and I can't get over it."[2] How true! We've thought about getting organized. We've read books, gone to classes, maybe even hired a consultant or helper. But nothing seems to change.

Certainly there's a need for change. No denying that. We look around every day and lament what we see. There's stuff everywhere; we encounter it constantly. We know that if we don't get organized we'll continue to be swamped in a morass of stuff. We earnestly believe the work is important. We know that organizing would make a big difference. But believing the work worthy of our effort doesn't get us organized either.

Contradiction Evokes Feeling; Feeling Evokes Awareness

When we experience the discontinuity between what we know and what we do, all kinds of uncomfortable feelings arise—shame, anger, frustration, sadness, despair. These powerful feelings make us vulnerable, touchy, and tender. We construct reasons and justifications to take away these emotions or at least soothe them. But it doesn't work. Instead, we forcibly damp down our feelings, muffle the conflicting voices, and hide the anguish from ourselves and others.

However, we need not squelch feeling in order to do what needs to be done. Instead, we can accept our feelings and, at the same time, develop our capacity to bear them. This is again a *both/and* situation, not *either/or*. It's a matter of acceptance, not willpower. We are both afraid and courageous, both clear and confused. We accept our feelings, we acknowledge their power . . . and take steps anyway.

Needleman shows that the dilemma of knowing what to do and yet not doing it has value we can hardly imagine. In the midst of the contradiction we approach "the gateway to consciousness of our true nature" where we stand in "the opposition between the inner movement toward the deep self and the outer movement toward the external world."[3] Through this gateway, we come to understand, deeply in our bones, our nature as beings of much more than rational knowing.

We are as much feeling and intuiting beings as thinking beings. We live in a world that is far more than the mental. Neither reasons, justifications, nor thoughts come near to explaining everything that's happening. When we stand in the uncomfortable experience of knowing yet not doing, we come closer to this reality. If stay with the discomfort, we find a depth in ourselves, a complexity that is more like who we really are.

The Habit of Thinking

Habitual thinking engages us constantly. We mull over past events, rehearse future ones, and mentally fiddle with the present. All this mental activity appears to "do" something, but in fact, it does very little and helps us avoid actually dealing with our stuff. To make something happen, we need to pull back from thinking and give more weight to doing.

This chapter and the Interludes throughout the book center on *thinking*—ideas, images, and insights that give form to thoughts about organizing, provide guidance, and trigger understanding. They give the thinking self something to do so that, soothed and occupied, it can get out of the way to give the doing self a turn. The skill chapters center on *doing*—the techniques, tools, and practice opportunities that bring organizational changes out into the world. The thinking/doing ratio in this book is about one part thinking to five parts doing. That's a reasonable ratio to shift away from habitual thinking toward a more balanced approach.

Resistance as Evidence of Movement

Poised on the brink of actually doing something about disorganization, not just thinking about it, resistance shows up. It may come in the form of a balky, angry "you can't make me!" attitude, or scattered anxiety that wants to bolt, running in wide-eyed panic from the scene. It may come as moralistic perfectionism that asks, "If I can't do this perfectly, why do it at all?" or shame at our lack of discipline, motivation, or willpower. It may come as dull, shut-down apathy, waves of fatigue, or feelings of laziness or embarrassment. When these powerful feelings come up, we suddenly find more important (or less important!) things to do. Confronting our resistance is just too much.

Resistance, however, is a sign that we are wrestling with an angel . . . or a formidable demon. It shows us that what we're about to attempt has the potential to make a real change in how we live our life. No wonder we resist!

When it comes right down to it, despite our resistance, we do want a life full of meaning and power. And for that, we wrestle with our resistance, learn the lessons it offers, and make peace with it. Throughout the organizing process we will encounter resistance again and again. Best that we honor resistance as an important messenger, get to know its particular forms, listen to what it has to say . . . and proceed.

The Mystery of Change

We might think we can't change; we've been like this for years. Yet, we do change all the time. Looking at photographs from former years, we see that once upon a time we loved red and wore it everywhere; now it's purple and blue. Once we were teachers; now we program computers. We've moved, remarried, had children, made new friends. Changing how we organize ourselves is just one change in a long string of changes, going back to the past and ahead to the future.

This particular change, however, seems different. Not so easy. Not so natural. We've tried getting organized before and it hasn't worked. Why should this attempt be any different? The point is—we don't know in advance if this approach, or any approach, will work.

Change is mysterious. We try to capture it, tame it, and bend it to our will, but it remains a mystery. Say we decide to change an old habit. We push and shove and try as hard as we can; if we don't get results, we may give up. Then somehow, mysteriously, we change. I'm reminded of when I quit smoking. Every New Year's Eve for five years, I made a resolution to quit. Sometimes I lasted a week, sometimes a few days, once even a month. Nothing seemed to work. I cut down, again and again. I must've "quit" fifty times. Then one year it happened. There wasn't much I could point to that was different, yet somehow the conditions were right. The last resolution stuck, and I never smoked again. A mystery!

Waiting for Change

Experience tells us that we don't necessarily change in the way and at the time we want to. Even though we may not know exactly what will bring about the shift that resolves the situation, we can, nonetheless, prepare for it, attend to it, and make it more likely. Back when I got frequent migraines, as the headache came on I would go into "help-the-headache" mode. I'd do slow neck rolls, massage my temples, tense and release my shoulder muscles. I would lay off sardines, chocolate, and peanuts, the very foods I wanted to eat. I would shade my eyes, put in earplugs, and drink warm water. None of this actually took away the migraine. They just made me more comfortable as I waited it out. Acupuncture finally shifted my neural circuits, yet the "help-the-headache" routine became part of my post-migraine life and, no doubt, contributed to making future headaches less frequent.

As we wait for the shift in how we organize to show up, there's much we can do. We can practice the skills in this book: clear the clutter, make things look and feel better, get rid of stuff. Not only do these activities soothe that part of us that just wants to do *something*, they both prepare the ground for the shift and at the same time actually address the distress.

The real shift—the one that fundamentally changes everything—is more a gift bestowed on us than something we consciously do. Legend tells us that the appearance of these shifts is often very modest. They don't come as heroic entries into the enemy castle accompanied by trumpets and drums. Deep shifts appear when we are able to receive them. The best we can do is keep our attention open and welcoming, focus on the intention, practice the skills, and trust that the shift is on its way. This time, the conditions may be right. This approach might click in. This might be exactly what will change us deeply and forever.

2. How to Use This Book

THE TWELVE SKILLS at the heart of this book give practical experience in getting organized. They can be used for any organizing situation—at home, at work, or in the community; with our papers, clothes, or files. Using the skills gives immediate, practical benefits: we have an organized desk, a streamlined wardrobe, or workable files. Using them also benefits our soul: our categories reflect our personal thought-patterns, our systems support sustainable engagement with the world, our organizing processes mirror the grand processes of Nature. Practicing these twelve skills makes our stuff the instrument of meaning and power.

The skills fall into two groups, those that operate in the visible world "out there" and those that operate in the spaces behind, between, and through the visible world. The Outer Skills deal directly with our stuff. The Inner Skills prepare, consolidate, and support what happens in the outer world.

THE SKILLS

Outer Skills:

- ✦ The Beginning and Ending Skills help us get in and out of organizing work effectively and gracefully.
- ✦ The Sorting, Staging, Storing, and Shedding Skills give shape to our environment: we gather stuff into categories, set up appropriate places to put stuff, and get rid of what we don't need.
- ✦ The Sustaining Skill helps us maintain our organizing system.

Inner Skills:

- ✦ The Observing and Acknowledging Skills bear witness to what happens as we organize; they help us gather information and get a sense of progress.

✦ The Imagining Skill opens up possibilities; the Choosing Skill narrows them down.

✦ The Engaging Skill makes connections between organizing and all other aspects of life.

The process of getting organized calls on both kinds of skills. As we do some Sorting, we will undoubtedly also be using Observing to note the pattern our stuff is taking. As we do Shedding, we use the Choosing Skill to make peace with what we leave behind. As we use the Sustaining Skill to maintain our systems, we are Engaging with our daily lives to give organizing its place in our schedule.

Everyday Skills, Spiritual Skills
Each of the skills is already familiar; we have a whole history of everyday experience with them to draw upon. Take Observing, for example. When we make a shopping list, we exercise the Observing Skill, noting the empty spot in the refrigerator where eggs usually are. We use the Acknowledging Skill when we give that satisfied sigh as we look upon the shiny floor we've just washed. We use Sorting and Staging when we lay out the dry laundry before putting it away. Such familiar, *everyday* uses of the skills open each chapter.

The skills also can be used in our spiritual life. For instance, Observing is the prime skill drawn upon in mindfulness meditation practices. Engaging helps us to sense our connection to all beings in the universe. Shedding helps us let go of spiritual practices that no longer serve us. The very skills we use when we organize the papers on our desks or the clothes in our closets are the same ones that we call on to develop spiritually. The *everyday* and *spiritual* uses of the skills open each chapter.

The body of each chapter explains the skill and demonstrates it with examples. Practice sheets after the explanation offer opportunities to exercise the skill. Throughout the chapter, cross-references below the butterflies in the margins point to material in other parts of the book relevant to the skill at hand. For example, in Sustaining we draw on Observing to see how long it takes to go through mail in order to make a reasonable maintenance schedule. In Ending, we also use Acknowledging to note the progress we've made in the session.

The Order of the Chapters
We start with the inner Witness Skills of Observing and Acknowledging, whereby we gather good data, promote a helpful point of view, and sense progress as it

occurs. Then we encounter the outer Threshold Skills, Ending and Beginning, by which we enter and exit the work gracefully.

Witness Skills—Observing and Acknowledging
Threshold Skills—Ending and Beginning

Before the hands-on Organizing Skills, an interlude—Structure in the Surface—gives a philosophical context to the process of perceiving patterns. The interlude lays the groundwork for the Shaping Skills of Sorting, Staging, Storing, and Shedding.

Interlude—Structure in the Surface
Shaping Skills—Sorting, Staging, Storing, and Shedding

Before the next group of skills, another interlude—the Interplay of Polarities—explores some spiritual and cultural dilemmas we encounter as we get organized. This interlude lays the groundwork for the Options Skills of Choosing and Imagining, which either close down or open up possibilities.

Interlude—The Interplay of Polarities
Skills for Handling Options—Choosing and Imagining

The last group, Skills to Carry On, Sustaining and Engaging, helps us maintain our organizing systems and put them in context on both the outer and inner levels.

Skills to Carry On—Sustaining and Engaging

The basic principles on which the skills depend are encapsulated in catchphrases listed at the end of that group's introduction. You will also see them appear throughout the text where they relate to other ideas. All of the catchphrase definitions—including some useful ones not specifically mentioned in the skill chapters—can be found in the catchphrase list at the back of the book *(see page 181)*.

Practice Sheets

The practice sheets in each chapter provide opportunities to apply the skill to the materials at hand in your home or office. Some are simple; some are complex. Some are particularly relevant to your situation; others may not be as much. Some are attractive and exciting; others may be daunting. The practice sheets are invitations to make physical changes, to perceive in a different way, to exercise focus, or to loosen your grip on tightly held ways of being.

You can use the practice sheets in a number of ways. Some you will ease into effortlessly. Some you might repeat using different materials, for example, first to sort papers and then to sort clothing. If you're put off by homework, you might skip them. You might, however, approach them as experiments or play, or invent your own. If you tend to "save up" practice sheets for the end of a session with the book, try starting with one instead. Loosening up your way of working allows new ways to emerge that may serve better than you'd assume.

Working with even a few practice sheets has impact far beyond the immediate task. For example, what we learn when we use Sorting to organize our desktop builds our capacity for Sorting the clothes in our closet and the food in our pantry. To develop one skill also helps us with others. For instance, Observing helps us with Staging and Storing. Acknowledging helps us with Sustaining and Shedding. It may seem that working on only a small area doesn't begin to address the "full catastrophe" (to quote Anthony Quinn in the movie, *Zorba the Greek*). However, work in one area ripples far beyond the immediate situation and supports the whole enterprise.

TRACKING THROUGH THE BOOK

This book is designed so you can follow wherever interest leads. You can start at page one and go through to the end or you can read the chapters in any order. You can browse the headings or dive in for detail, look up catchphrases or consult the index for related material. You can also take whatever sidetracks present themselves in the margin cross-references. These will appear with a butterfly icon whenever there are opportunities for you to revisit previous material or check out something up ahead that applies to the topic you are currently reading. As the butterfly flies from flower to flower, so the mind follows interest. The margin cross-references allow the mind to follow where it is led, going with its tendency to associate.

My intention for this self-help book is that it will change your life, period. If you're one of those people who want to do hands-on work right now, I encourage you, in fact urge you, to jump ahead to the Shaping Skills chapters. That's where you'll find specific suggestions to get you going. Taking the chapters in order, however, provides a context for those skills.

Regardless of the route, you'll probably encounter most of the material via the cross-references. All roads lead to the same destination; how you get there is up to you. You might actually skip chapters or read them in part. Not everything in this book is equally important to every person. You need to trust that what attracts you is what you need to pay attention to.

Following the Heart's Desire

Following attraction is the surest way to get whatever it is we want. Whether we acknowledge it or not, each one of us knows, better than anyone else possibly could, what our heart's desire is. At first, we may not have a clue. However, we can put ourselves in a position to let desire show up.

The tracker, following an elusive deer through the wild, recognizes the signs—scraped trunks, broken twigs, hoof marks pointing in a certain direction. At dusk when the deer is likely to pass, the tracker is in position for an encounter. So, we begin to track our desire. We recognize subtle signs of interest and give desire some open space in which to appear.

Here is a simple exercise using the Table of Contents that gives desire an opportunity to reveal itself. Scan the chapter titles and note which attract and which don't, which bring up anxiety and which are neutral. These are the traces of desire and interest, both positive and negative. If we follow the track, we'll get what we're looking for. Some will want to follow the attraction; other brave souls will want to follow the anxiety. Surprisingly, both tracks work.

When we go off the straight track, we might worry that we're missing something. In this book, however, that's unlikely, since access to all of the material can come through any one of the parts. The concepts and practices are interconnected and interdependent. Learning about one skill helps all the others make sense; working a practice sheet from one skill develops facility with other skills. As in a holographic image, the entire picture is present in any piece of it. The more pieces we have, the stronger the picture.

Kindly Interest

A helpful attitude to take is one of curious, kindly interest, not just to the nuts-and-bolts of practice sheets and explanations but also to the feelings going on inside.

This attitude is explored in the Witness Skill chapters, Observing and Acknowledging. We can expect to be uncomfortable at first. We might feel anxious, awkward, or mistrustful of our ability to make any difference at all. We might be concerned with doing it right. We might feel sad, ashamed, or frustrated. All these emotions crowd in and try to grab us by the throat.

At these moments, kindly interest offers some breathing space. We give ourselves leave to feel the distress without shutting down. At the same time, we take a slight step back from the distress to attend to the lessons it presents. Even in our anxiety, we see that arranging our space according to how we work makes it easier to remember where things are. Even though we feel awkward going through the steps of wrapping up a session of organizing work, we notice later that organizing doesn't haunt us so much when we're away from it.

When we allow ourselves the difficult emotions and at the same time do what needs doing, we can respond with creativity, flexibility, and appropriateness. Change is difficult, disorienting, and upsetting. The more we foster kindly interest in what happens as it happens, the easier it is for change to take hold.

Process As Much As Product

Organizing is an ongoing process that ebbs and flows. Occasionally we give it special attention. We learn about new approaches and try them out. We achieve certain goals, such as organizing a closet or desk, or setting up a filing system. At such times, organizing is in the foreground of our attention and activity. After the task is done, we let organizing recede into the background, where it serves as an ever-present support to whatever we're doing. This process is explored in the Skills to Carry On—Sustaining and Engaging.

Because life continually evolves, there is always something more to do, even if we have achieved a level of accomplishment. The recitalist basks in the applause, yet knows that tomorrow there's another piece to learn. The athlete, even with gold medal in hand, knows there's another level of mastery to achieve. Organizing isn't done once and for all, but rather, like life, is open-ended. Certainly there are accomplishments and resting points along the way, but there is always more beneath, above, behind, or within to explore. Organizing is process as well as product.

STUFF AS THE INSTRUMENT; SKILLS AS THE PRACTICE

Getting organized is like bringing a piece of music out into the world. The musical notes of a symphonic score are marks on a page that suggest the beauty and emotional impact of a full-blown symphony. Until the piece is played, however, the notes are just marks. When the orchestra members play their instruments, the sounds latent in the piece come out into the world for everyone to hear. Then the symphony becomes "real."

Just as the players' instruments allow the symphony to be heard, so our stuff allows our life to be experienced in the material world. Stuff is the "instrument" by which we work out the patterns latent in our life and give them meaning. We recognize what's going on inside us and bring it forth into the world.

For example, we might know that nurturing relationships with friends feeds our soul. We can use our stuff to reflect how we feel about friends: we display their greeting cards or artwork, we clear our calendar for them, we contain other stuff that competes for our attention. All of these actions bring friendship into the foreground.

As we work with our papers, books, and clothes, the patterns operating deep within us come forth. We see before us our history, our aspirations, and the particular agenda our soul has in store for us. We become present to ourselves through our stuff, the instrument we play in the symphony of life.

Resonance

When we're disorganized, our cluttered, chaotic surroundings are out of sync with our desire for a rich spiritual life or our urge to exert influence in the world. What we're trying to do in the world seems to have little effect, like the wave coming into shore that's canceled out by the wave behind it whose pattern of crest-and-trough is out of sync. As we get organized, our inner and outer "environments" begin to relate harmoniously, like wave patterns that reinforce each other. With the inner and outer in resonant relationship, power is born. We make decisions, move forward, and change. We ring like a bell.

Practice

Getting organized is a practice that develops gradually, over time. When we start out, the work is uncomfortable, tedious, or even embarrassing. For example, practicing the Sorting Skill can be excruciating the first time we try. We'd rather run off to any distraction: the ringing phone, the creative idea we'd much rather pursue, even other organizing tasks. Instead, we name each item's category as it presents itself without getting involved in the associations the item brings up. After four or five sessions of conscious Sorting, we feel we've been using the skill all our life. Just as we don't expect a beginning violinist to pick up the instrument and play like a concertmaster, so we allow ourselves to be beginners at organizing. As we develop facility, the quality of our practice shifts, becoming richer, more widely applicable, and more satisfying.

Just as some instruments are difficult to play and others are easy, so we each have a unique set of stuff to deal with—some have mountains of stuff, others just need a filing system. Just as some players are naturally gifted, and others aren't, so some of us have natural ability with organizing, others have little talent for it, nor models, nor experience. Anyone, however, with an appropriate instrument, understanding of the principles, good guidance, and practice can make music of some sort, even if it's drumming on the steering wheel, or whistling. So it is with organizing. Regardless of our particular challenges or abilities, we can, with appropriate tools, skills, understanding, guidance, and conscious practice, become organized.

A Spiritual Practice

Most activities, if pursued over time, provide a metaphor that can contain virtually any thought, emotion, sensation, or belief. They mirror our experience back to us, giving it form and meaning. Music can provide the metaphor, as can gardening, fishing, climbing the corporate ladder, or keeping house. These activities connect us with the mysteries of our souls and are, in fact, our spiritual practice. Getting organized can be a spiritual practice as well. Through it we come face to face with the deepest, broadest issues in life—when to hold on and when to let go; what to value and what not to value; who we are, have been, and who we would like to be.

The First and Only Lesson

I didn't know it at the time, but my best piano teacher taught me everything I would learn from her in the first lesson. Or would have, had I been able to take it in. The principles were few and simple. Practicing them, on the other hand, has been a lifetime pursuit. As with playing piano, there are only a few basic principles that carry everything we need to know about getting organized. This handbook lays them out. Every time we encounter them, they settle at a different level. We may well return here again and again, perhaps over the course of a lifetime.

More Words on Resistance

With all these musical metaphors in this book, you'd think I was a "natural" at it. But no. I struggle with an on-again/off-again relationship with music. My path had as much doubt and discouragement as satisfaction and joy. I've had to work with technical limitations and plough through resistance and inertia. Luckily I found some worthy teachers, so I am competent, knowledgeable, and quite good, even. I'm not great, and will never be.

Not being a "natural" is a real advantage, though, when helping others. I remember struggling with a knotty piano passage, far beyond what I could do easily. I went to my good buddy in the practice room next door. "Help! I'm stuck, I can't play this." She looked at it, and, being a natural, said, "Oh, that," as the notes rippled off her fingers. "Thanks," I said weakly, and went back to my room no wiser.

I've had plenty of personal struggles trying to do something "unnatural" in my own life, so I can heartily empathize with those who struggle with organization. I consider myself right in the middle between being awkward and being a "natural" when it comes to getting organized. The middle position is a good place for those like me who hope to help. After all, the naturals at organization aren't reading this book. Those who struggle are.

Witness Skills
Developing a Point of View

IN OUR FAST-PACED, overwhelmingly chaotic environment, the most helpful thing we can do is develop some perspective. The Witness Skills, Observing and Acknowledging, help us do just that. In the midst of our busy lives, we disengage slightly from our situation to establish a point from which we can view the situation—a point of calm amidst charged feelings, obsessive thoughts, and frantic activity.

We foster a welcome and necessary measure of detachment through Observing, yet at the same time maintain presence and purpose through Acknowledging. The detachment of Observing differs from dissociation. In dissociation, we protectively absent ourselves from a situation. Here we become exquisitely present. Observing takes note of feelings, thoughts, and results. Acknowledging puts our observations in context, gathering useful feedback about what helps or hinders us. Using Witness Skills, we merely note; we don't criticize, ruminate, or worry. When we establish this viewpoint, panic, frustration, and obsession recede. We loosen the vise-grip by which we try to maintain control and allow some space for new ways of being to arise.

The Witness Skills put us in touch with both parts of our selves—that which is involved in the outer world of doing, and that which is involved in inner world of being. The Witness Skills help us mediate between the two, fostering an easy flow between what goes on inside us and what goes on around us. If nothing else comes from reading this book, the capacity to maintain this inner/outer relationship would be enough.

WITNESS SKILL CATCHPHRASES

Eagle View/Ant View
Foreground/Background
Reality Check   *(See page 181 for definitions.)*

Everyday Observing

We use Observing when we

> assemble a shopping list by noting what's missing in the refrigerator
>
> note that we have a headache and take an aspirin
>
> observe our irritation when we're cut off in traffic
>
> take note of landmarks when navigating in unknown territory

Spiritual Observing

We use Observing when we

> step back from a distressing situation and notice our thoughts, feeling, or breathing
>
> notice things in our environment that relate to our thoughts, and vice versa
>
> notice patterns in what we experience
>
> notice clues and signs that orient us to our life purpose

3. Observing

Gathering Data

OBSERVING SEEMS so innocuous, so simple. Merely noticing what's happening—what a nonskill! We do Observing every day: we observe the weather and dress accordingly; we observe the absence of sharp pencils and go sharpen some; we observe how much time is left before we have to leave and move toward the door.

A SIMPLE YET POWERFUL SKILL

The skill of Observing—gathering data about ourselves and our surroundings—supports the work of all organizing skills. For example, when we observe which of our projects are active, which are on hold, and which are coming up, we support the work of Staging. When we identify the next step in an organizing process before we disengage from it, we support the work of Ending. When we observe what tasks are necessary to maintain our systems, we support the work of Sustaining.

If this were all Observing offered, it would be valuable enough. However, as important as the data is the point of view from which the observations are made. Observing establishes a viewpoint that is, paradoxically, both in the midst of our situation and slightly apart from it.

The Second Self

Observing establishes a "second self"—a presence that parallels the thinking, doing, feeling self. This second self is what's called upon in spiritual practices, such as when we "watch and pray," or meditate on the breath. The second self, or the observer, doesn't plan the next organizing task or feel the remorse of finding a particularly neglected area to organize. It doesn't do the work either. The observer merely, and fully, observes.

The Curious Anthropologist, Not the Judge

Like the curious anthropologist, the observer is interested in everything without regard to preferences, expectations, or judgments. The anthropologist wouldn't say, "Yuck, they eat that smelly stuff for breakfast!" S/he would simply note, "The inhabitants of this island have fermented taro root for their first meal." The observer lets the data—thoughts, feeling, actions, situations—be noticed as they are, without a spin of judgment.

Judgments—about what we should do, about what other people think, about how we ought to feel—limit Observing. They filter the data coming in so we cease to notice everything that's there. In fact, the judge is more likely to focus on what's not working rather than what is, just to confirm its judgments.

For example, we might want fewer clothes lying around our bedroom and so ask our observer to gather data for us. The nonjudgmental observer notices that mostly the larger, bulky items like sweaters and jackets are left out, not socks and underwear. We can then zero in on making a better storage space for the big items. If our observer is a judge, all it notices is that "clothes are lying around, and that's bad," period. The judge leaves us with a vague negative feeling, rather than specific data supporting a plan of action.

In performance, if the pianist's observer is stuck in the judge role, every "wrong" note looms large, instead of merely being filed away with other reminders of passages to work on. Indeed, s/he risks total breakdown of the performance if the judge takes over. Similarly, when we try to get organized, our judge can stop us cold, saying we're doing it wrong or we should've done this years ago or we'll never get it right.

The nonjudgmental observer looks on with eager, fascinated interest, letting nothing slip by. It notes the entire range of circumstances, whether we deem them good or bad, simple or complicated, helpful or hindering. It reports; it does not censor, filter, or crticize.

Can We Stand It?

What we observe isn't always pleasant. We observe piles of unopened mail on the kitchen counter, a filing drawer so full it can't take one more paper, a closet we can hardly get into for all the stuff on the floor blocking our way. In the face of these observations we might feel shame, embarrassment, anger, or impatience. We might concoct elaborate excuses, rationalizations, and justifications for our situation. We might sadly yearn for the environment we wish we had. So we stop observing; it's just too painful.

Right here is the challenge—to be able to stand what we observe. Not in a tough-it-out way, but in a curious-anthropologist way. If we can stand it, even for a few seconds, we've got an open space in which to work. We begin to take an interest in what's going on, rather than drowning in emotions or fabricating reasons.

We can use the data feelings give us to shape the course of our organizing work. For instance, observing the anxiety that comes up when we encounter an unpaid bill while sorting papers can steer us to set up a reliable bill-paying system. Observing the sadness that arises when we get rid of clothing we'll never fit into leads us to respect our grief and, ultimately, helps us let go more thoroughly. Observing our relief at locating last year's tax return encourages us to continue revamping our files.

Standing in our feelings, even for a brief moment, gives our life grounding and validation. If we feel frustrated, so be it. If we feel discouraged, so be it. If we feel elated (especially!) so be it. With good Observing Skills we can honor the tough times (almost) as much as the times when the work flows well. Physical reality becomes something to work with, rather than struggle against. Nonjudgmental Observing propels us into unconditional engagement with life. We welcome it all.

OBSERVING IN ACTION

The observing point-of-view is available to us at any time. We summon it by consciously taking the smallest step back from the situation we're immersed in, while at the same time maintaining open attention. Both stepping back and opening the attention can be cultivated. Although it's easy to be completely caught up in our situation, it is possible to step back if we take that step consciously and willfully. We can also protect our attention from pressing thoughts or feelings, giving the observations space in which to present themselves.

As we disengage, "the observing self," says Arthur Deikman in his book by the same name, "emerges with increasing clarity and stability, while the observed world of emotions, thoughts, and sensations becomes correspondingly less compelling, less dictatorial, and unquestioned."[4] First attempts at Observing are often pale and fleeting. However, the more we take up the Observing point of view and attend to whatever it has to offer, the more strength and stamina we develop.

Observing can be seen as a four-stage process: we step out of the stream of experience, open our attention, capture whatever information presents itself, and step back into the stream—all done in a moment. We catch observations on the fly, as we go about our business.

Stage 1. Step out of the stream:

When we first try to consciously step out of the stream of experience, it might take a supreme act of will—like halting ourselves in a slide down a slippery slope. Unlike the deer and dog, who have no choice but to be caught up in the stream of life, we can consciously direct our attention. Even in the midst of distress and high drama, we can disengage slightly from our experience. We might even take a physical step back and let our eyes take in a wider view.

Stage 2. Open the attention:

We then open our attention to whatever presents itself. Thoughts and feelings about the situation we're trying to observe might crowd in. However, we can give our observer a little space in which to work by taking a slow breath and setting thoughts aside. The observing point of view is similar to that we use when taking measurements; it's just information, we don't get emotionally involved. In the beginning, our observations might seem few and insignificant, but as we develop our observing presence, more observations will present themselves.

Stage 3. Capture the information:

Then we capture the data. This step might be as simple as merely taking note of a physical arrangement. For example, we observe that we like to work in a spot that has a view. Or we note that our energy for organizing fades after about ten minutes of work. Capturing the information might require some advance preparation. For example, we might have sticky-notes at hand to capture the names of the categories when we sort papers. Notepads and even tape- or video recorders can be useful in capturing information.

Stage 4. Step back into the stream:

When we have the data we need, we return to the experience. The observing point of view comes and goes. We don't stay in it, but move through it. Oftentimes the little sojourn in Observing can give welcome relief from a distressing situation. We find that even in the midst of the storm, there is an island of calm.

Forgetting to Observe

We might have every intention to observe—even such a simple thing as how long it takes to leave the house. Then, all of a sudden, we find ourselves in the car driving away. Oops! We get caught up in the stream of life or involved in the drama of our situation. If we forget, we do have the option of observing after the fact. We take a moment to replay the scene, open our attention to whatever comes up, capture that information, or at least make a good guess, and step back into the stream of experience.

Gifts of Observing

Observing alerts us to useful information that supports our organizing work. For example, we observe how often we go through the mail, which helps us make a realistic schedule. We observe where we pay the bills and so set up a workspace there. We observe what colors we like so our organizing tools are inviting. We observe our frustration when we misplace our keys and so decide to establish a "parking place" for them

See Sustaining, page 157.

See Staging, page 85.

Observing can also give us valuable information about our habits. As we get familiar with habitual responses, we have a chance to recognize what's going on and do something different next time. Most urges, if we can bear them for a while, pass on their own. Changing habits, then, rests not so much on willpower as on our ability to observe when and how habits kick in. We can then open up a space for a different response. Since much organizing distress comes from habits—bringing in more than we need, not putting things away, or piling things in a heap—the Observing Skill is especially valuable. We notice the particulars of the distress without getting immersed in it.

From this vantage point we might see that, in the greater scheme of things, what seemed unhelpful may turn out to be perfectly appropriate. For example, my habit of going to the kitchen whenever I run into a snag might be a way to gain necessary distance, rather than an escape. With that in mind, the trip to the kitchen helps me continue working, as long as I don't browbeat myself or eat something bad.

As we find meaning in our madness, we're encouraged to observe even more. We slip into and out of the observing point of view at will. Observing is but a hair's breadth away. All we need do is step out of the stream of experience, set aside attachment, and look at things as they are.

Observing on the Fly

The intent of this exercise is to give you a readily accessible experience of the observing self in the midst of another activity, in this case, reading the practice sheet. Keep the exercise emotionally neutral. Merely report—don't rehearse, reflect, judge, or classify.

Allow yourself, right at this moment, to observe with each of your senses—touch (both external and internal), taste, smell, hearing, and sight—while you read this practice sheet.

Note:

the temperature of the room and any movement of air . . . [keep reading] . . .

any physical sensations in your body . . . [keep reading] . . .

any taste in your mouth . . . [keep reading] . . .

the smells in the air . . . [keep reading] . . .

any ambient sound that drifts in . . . [keep reading] . . .

the quality of light on the page . . . [keep reading] . . .

The trick is to keep doing what you're doing, which in this case is reading. At first, you might feel a need to stop what you're doing in order to observe. That's fine in the beginning. As Observing becomes more accessible, you'll find less and less need to stop. Soon you will be able to move into Observing and out again in a heartbeat.

List some observations below:

_____

_____

_____

_____

Some observations are easier to notice than others; note that difference. Try this exercise in different venues—as you walk down the street, from your door to the car, entering a store, while in conversation.

Reality Check

People who have trouble with organizing often don't have a reliable sense of how long things take. They say, "oh, it'll only take a few minutes." A half-hour later they're still at it. Noting actual clock time—when you start a task and when you're done with it—establishes a benchmark to get you firmly grounded in reality.

When you do a reality check, you're gathering data like the curious anthropologist, not judging against some theoretical ideal. With sound data in hand you can then use other skills to make whatever changes your observations suggest.

Honor how things actually go. For example, putting the groceries away might take ten minutes by itself. However, other factors need to be taken in account: you might need to set up something to occupy your child while you work, you might need to let the dog out first, or you might get a phone call that takes your attention.

Take your reality check in context. Glance at a timepiece before you start a task and after you've finished. Note the actual elapsed time. Use this sheet for practice now and when you work with Shaping Skill practice sheets later on in the book.

Task		Total	
	Time Start	Time End	Time Elapsed
Getting dressed	_____	_____	_____
Going to bed	_____	_____	_____
(Fill in your own tasks)			
_____	_____	_____	_____
_____	_____	_____	_____
_____	_____	_____	_____
_____	_____	_____	_____

Everyday Acknowledging

We use Acknowledging when we

fill up the gas tank and feel secure, having plenty of fuel

look in the mirror as we arrange our hair

feel the effects of an exercise session—increased heartbeat, sweating, heavy breathing

decline a second helping of food, satisfied with what we have

Spiritual Acknowledging

We use Acknowledging when we

pay attention to how our behavior matches our intention when we decide to change a habit

use our interactions with people, animals, and the natural world to acknowledge connections

participate in weddings and funerals with conscious connection to our communal past

notice and act on signs from the world around and within us that orient us spiritually

4. Acknowledging
Placing Value

IN ACKNOWLEDGING we're not just searching for data, any data, as we are in Observing. We're sensing forward motion, progress, or accomplishment. It's Observing with a purpose. As in Observing, our sensors are in search mode, open to what we see, hear, or run into "out there," or what we feel physically, emotionally, or intuitively "in here." Beyond merely gathering data, however, we are identifying and naming the value of what we observe.

See Observing, page 21

MAKING PROGRESS

One of the greatest challenges in getting organized is sensing, right from the beginning, that what we do has value, that our efforts make a difference, that we're making progress. When there's so much to do, our small efforts don't seem to have an effect. It's like when we were young and Mom put a huge plate of spaghetti before us and said, "Now, be sure to clean your plate!" We looked at the spaghetti and thought, "This is impossible. There's no way I can eat all of this." But, dutifully, we dove in. We ate and ate and ate, one forkful after another, but it didn't seem to make any difference. There seemed to be just as much spaghetti as before. Still, we kept at it, forkful by forkful, until, miraculously, we could see a little bit more plate and a little bit less spaghetti. Finally we could sense that we were making progress. Each one of those forkfuls had an effect, although it didn't seem so at the time. Acknowledging is the skill that helps us sense that what we do makes a difference. It validates our efforts, honors the reality of what's happening, and gives it value.

ACKNOWLEDGING, REGARDLESS

When we first start organizing, whatever we do might not seem like much. Our tolerance for organizing may be embarrassingly low—ten minutes of work might be all we can muster. The work is unfamiliar; we're awkward, inefficient, and just not good at it. We're emotionally uncomfortable, we feel the shame of not having done this long ago, or are angry that we have to deal with this stuff at all. It's no wonder what we do appears so insignificant.

See
Sorting,
page 75

Yet there's more to acknowledge than the few papers we've managed to sort, or the few clothes we've shed. We're embarking on a new way of operating. We're exercising new skills. That we did it at all is certainly worth acknowledging.

There are also side benefits to our work. For instance, when we sort, not only do we end up with papers in categories, we also get to know what our categories are. Our thinking shapes up as much as our stuff. The next time we sort, we'll already have categories in hand. So, we can also acknowledge the change in our thinking process and the benefits for future sessions.

Acknowledging Along the Way

We often neglect giving ourselves credit until the job is completely done. This habit not only sets us up for discouragement but also denies the facts of the matter. We were there, we did some work, and we had an effect. Intermediate goals, not just the final product, are worthy of acknowledgment. If we deny ourselves legitimate credit for work in progress, we'll get exactly one pat on the back—just before we step into the grave. Most tasks are works in progress; few are ever done once and for all. The more we go with how life actually happens, the more supported by reality we become. Acknowledging early and often fosters not only a sense of accomplishment but also an atmosphere of eagerness to continue and make more changes.

Push Back the "Yes, But . . ."

At the first meeting of my classes, participants talk about their issues with organization. One man went on about how every morning he struggles to find a matching pair of socks. The evidence was before us—he lifted his pant legs to reveal one blue sock and one brown.

At the next session, he reported at the progress check-in, "Well, I haven't done much. I straightened up my sock drawer, but there's the whole back bedroom to organize and . . ." I interrupted him, asking, "Please say that again and stop before the 'but.'" He didn't quite get it, but said slowly, "Well, I haven't done much. I straightened up my sock drawer." As he repeated the sentence, he looked around at everyone's big smiles and finally realized *he had straightened up his sock drawer*—something he had been struggling with for years.

It is all too easy to say, "Yes, but there are still all these other things to do."

Thoughts of what's yet to be done command our attention. We need to protect what we've already done from the onslaught of what's yet to do. If we put up a clear boundary between the two, our legitimate accomplishments won't be compromised. With the boundary in place, we're encouraged to continue.

See Beginning, page 53

Satisfaction

In our fast-paced culture we keep looking to the next thing, and the next, and the next. Thus we miss the satisfaction that comes from acknowledging *this* accomplishment, here and now. When we clear up that nasty pile staring us in the face as we enter our office, we acknowledge the change rather than ricocheting our attention to the next organizing task. We pause a moment, look at the clear space, and feel how good it is to have a peaceful view. Acknowledging breeds ongoing, healthy satisfaction that reinforces positive effects and keeps us motivated.

Satisfaction comes from worthy efforts well acknowledged. The standard by which we designate our efforts worthy is a choice. Our criteria need not come from received messages that say that only a finished job is worthy of acknowledgment. We can frame criteria more in line with reality. Every single time we lend energy to organizing, something happens, something worth acknowledging.

THE SHADOW SIDE OF PROGRESS

Although there are times when we don't acknowledge legitimate progress, there are other times when we make so-called progress an end in itself. The General Electric television ads of the '50s said, "Progress is our most important product." We tick off items on our to-do list, even though they're peripheral tasks, just to feel accomplishment. The important, complicated, core tasks remain undone. We are like the Red Queen in Alice in Wonderland, running as fast as we can to stay in the same place. There may be furious activity, but no real progress. At the end of the day, what have we done?

Progress in itself is not an absolute good. Many spiritual paths don't, in fact, acknowledge progress as such but see instead a cycle of continually recurring events. Others take the spiral as their model, recurring, but within a context of a direction. Nonetheless, we have the urge to evolve. Humans have a sense of linear time. We can imagine our history—what came before and what might come after. Because of this time sense, we want to feel like we're making headway. We want to notice the difference. We want things to be better.

When we temper the urge toward progress as an end in itself and, at the same time, feed back to ourselves the real progress we've made, we honor the reality of the situation. We reflect on our experience—the challenges as well as the satisfactions. Acknowledging helps us look at things unconditionally, as they are.

Focus on What Works, As Well As What Doesn't

We are used to paying attention to what's not working rather than what is. When we get up in the morning we rarely say, "Gee, my left elbow feels so good!" We're more likely to say, "Oh, my right elbow hurts!" Difficulties, problems, and pains alert us to conditions that need to be addressed. Paying attention to what's not working is useful.

However, at the same time, there's a whole set of things that *are* working, that go along smoothly, and are just fine the way they are. What's working seems to pale before the drama of the difficulties. In Acknowledging we charge up what's working so it has as much presence as what's not. We lend energy and attention to the qualities we value and the actions we want to foster, and we withdraw attention from the rest.

Acknowledging lets our experience sink in and swirl around within us. If we ignore the entire range of lessons our experience presents to us, we find ourselves encountering the same lessons again and again. Better to acknowledge all that our experience brings. Then we may be more able to move forward.

Attending to the Negative

As youngsters we probably were made more aware of times when we fell short than times when we measured up. We're used to navigating negatively, avoiding or eliminating what's wrong, rather than going toward what's right. Consequently, we pay attention to what's "bad" while ignoring what's "good."

In her herbal books, Susun Weed *(for more information, see Resources, page 191)* contrasts the heroic focus on what's not working with the more subtle focus on what is. The hero rides in, slaying the "what's not working" dragon with the flashy, dramatic cure. The wise old woman on the other hand, quietly nurtures what's already healthy and allows it to flourish. If we shift the focus from eliminating pain to promoting wholeness, we foster what's working rather than what's not.

Do We Deserve It? Are We Entitled?

Many of us can hardly call forth the good things we do. It's uncomfortable, even

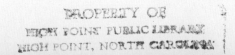

embarrassing. When we do manage to own our good work, we qualify it and play it down. We squirm when someone praises us; we're uncomfortable acknowledging even our legitimate accomplishments. We've been told that such attention is selfish or "tooting our own horn."

Our commercial culture toys with this sense of what we deserve. The "you deserve this" messages we pick up from advertising seem to say that we are only deserving because we suffer so much. We've worked so hard, we're so stressed out, so of course, we deserve it. The more we suffer, or think we suffer, the more entitled we feel to whatever it is we want. Linking our self-worth to suffering makes suffering a condition for deserving anything. We miss the fact that acknowledgment is available to us, unconditioned, at every turn. We can look dispassionately at our efforts and see in them, always, something worthy, whether we've suffered or not.

ACKNOWLEDGING KEEPS US ON TRACK

Acknowledging provides feedback that keeps us on track. The exercise in chapter 2 *(see page 13)* about noting which chapters held attraction for us shows feedback in action. We acknowledge what draws us onward and what stops us cold. We acknowledge what motivates us and what turns us off. Through Acknowledging we develop a sense that keeps us on the right track.

Musicians develop a similar sense. Usually they have only one lesson a week; the rest of the time they're on their own, shaping their daily practice by relying on their own feedback. Their ability to give themselves feedback can contribute as much to their playing ability as their natural talent. In performance, the pianist, while fully engaged in playing, also listens to the music as it flows forth. One note may come out louder than ever before, which, when s/he repeats the melody, s/he again emphasizes. That single note might even trigger a deep understanding of the piece s/he had never considered, making the performance fresh and alive.

As we get organized and make changes in our environment, we acknowledge how the new way of operating feels. Does it feel "right"? Am I learning to recognize what "right" is? Our body tells us that the new filing cabinet arrangement makes it physically easier to retrieve files. Our emotions tell us that the new arrangement settles down our "where is it?" anxiety. This is how Acknowledging orients us to stay on track.

Acknowledging Regardless

It is possible to find something worth acknowledging in everything you do. In this exercise, identify (in the moment, or after the fact) what is worthwhile in everyday activities. This sheet sensitizes your "antennae" so that when you call on Acknowledging in organizing situations, you'll have the skill in hand.

Remember, there's always something to acknowledge. In a phone call, although you may not get the information you need, you have determined that the person doesn't have it. When shopping, although you don't get the perfect gift, you are narrowing down the choices. In balancing your checkbook, even though it may not work out to the penny, you have determined that most of the checks are accurately recorded.

List things to acknowledge in these situations:

Phone call:

_____

_____

An encounter:

_____

_____

Looking in the mirror:

_____

_____

On a shopping trip:

_____

_____

What Attracts Me? What Moves Me? What Soothes Me?

Acknowledging helps us identify when we're on, when there's forward impetus, when energy flows. We note what charges us, what comforts us, what satisfies us, what gives us joy, inspiration, meaning, and connection.

Use this practice sheet over the course of a day or several days to acknowledge, in the moment or after the fact, what draws you onward. This information gets your "antennae" sensitized to what will help you when you make organizing choices.

What attracts me? (Think of many different qualities—examples of texture, temperature, color, materials, style of music, tempo, timing and rhythm, sounds, specific activities, and so on, that you like.)

_____

_____

_____

What moves me? (Think of situations where you've been stuck—what has gotten you off the mark? Examples might be: the baby crying, a glorious day, knowing that someone else will see what I'm doing, or not doing.)

_____

_____

_____

What soothes me? (Think of times when you've been anxious or desperate, what has helped and made a difference in your mood? Examples might be: beautiful music, lying down, a kind word from a friend, a vigorous walk.)

_____

_____

_____

Acknowledging Elsewhere

Practice sheets in other skill chapters rely heavily on the Acknowledging Skill. Look to these chapters for more practice:

Threshold Skills
Getting Into and Out of Organizing

CROSSING THRESHOLDS is scary business. We leave the familiar behind and step into the unknown. We're especially vulnerable and open to influences, and so need special techniques and protection. Transition ceremonies attest to that. Initiations mark a child's entry into adulthood, weddings begin a marriage, funerals carry people from life into death. Ancient spiritual traditions recognize the power of thresholds, boundaries, and edges with special deities and rites. Hermes (one of the most enigmatic of the Greek gods), Terminus (his more ancient counterpart), and Hecate (the feared crone) were worshipped at boundaries and borders.

The threshold place is fraught with feeling. People cry at weddings as well as funerals. There is grief in letting old ways go, as well as joyful anticipation of what's to come. There is hope and anxiety, courage and despair.

THE ORGANIZING THRESHOLD

When we're about to cross into getting organized, legions of distressing emotions loom large. We long for the organized environment we want but do not have. We are disgusted by our disorganization. We despair at the enormity of the task. We grieve at leaving our old, familiar, disorganized way behind. We fear our efforts won't show the quality we've come to expect of ourselves. Faced with such distressing emotions, we busy ourselves with something else, anything else—something easier, not so scary, not so important.

Because transitions seem so formidable, we submit willingly (in a way) to the alarm clock and the reveille bugle. If we didn't have the alarm, would we get up? Procrastination serves as an "alarm clock" as well. We wait until the very last minute, then plunge in, eyes squeezed shut. When we open our eyes, there we are, inside. We make it so we absolutely *have to* cross over, and then we do. In a way, of course, this works. Procrastination, however, exacts a toll on the body that is ultimately not sustainable.

Awareness Helps

When we shut our eyes at the threshold, we miss something important. Transition moments are exactly when magic happens. How do we cross over? It's a mystery. If we use our Threshold Skills and keep our true desire to change before us, we will be drawn with full awareness across the border. What helps is to open our eyes wider, not squeeze them shut.

In tracking, the act of moving from forest to field is delicate. Rather than charging into the open, the tracker pauses at the edge of the forest, becoming exquisitely attuned to the field—scanning near and far, sniffing, feeling the wind, listening. Entering, s/he leaves no "wake," but slips in, unnoticed. Having crossed over, s/he again pauses and lets the energy settle back down in the field where s/he has just become a participant.

The Threshold Skills offer ways to pass gracefully and effectively into and out of organizing. We pause at the edge, finding the most effective entry point. After we're through with our organizing session, we exit gracefully so that we will be welcomed back when we return. We make clear boundaries so that organizing won't haunt us when we're doing something else, and other tasks won't haunt us while organizing.

Boundaries

Boundary issues come up not only at the threshold but also throughout the process of organizing. We make clear boundaries between what we can and cannot do, between what we bring in and what we leave behind, between what we choose and what we reject. At times we draw the boundary in close; at other times we're inclusive and open. Boundaries are necessary for a being to function—bodies have skin, cells have walls, just as paintings have frames and symphonies begin and end. When boundaries are clear, strong, and healthy, organizing systems can thrive. The Threshold Skills take us into organizing with a focus on boundaries.

ORDER OF THE THRESHOLD SKILLS

The Ending Skill ensures that we won't get lost in the realm of organizing and can find our way out when we choose. Many of us need that assurance before we start, so in the order of the Threshold Skills, Ending comes first. The Beginning Skill identifies the not-so-secret passageway by which we make an effective entry into organizing. Both skills draw on the Witness Skills, Observing and Acknowledging, to direct and honor our work.

THRESHOLD SKILL CATCHPHRASES

End with Grace

From This Moment On

Plate of Spaghetti

Reality Check

Rope It Off

Start Small

(See page 181 for definitions.)

Everyday Ending

We use Ending when we

    close out a telephone call or a conversation at a party

    shut down the computer

    lock the door when we leave the house

    take the laundry out of the dryer and put it away

    take out the garbage

Spiritual Ending

We use Ending when we

    ritually end a relationship, returning items

    mark the passing phases of life, such as a child leaving home
    for college, a death, a job change

    review the day, prepare for tomorrow, and go into sleep

    honor seasonal changes by putting away outdoor furniture
    with conscious intention

5. Ending
Gracefully Disengaging from the Work

MANY PEOPLE FEEL that if they touch just one of those things-to-be-organized, they'll be stuck organizing for hours or all weekend or perhaps for the rest of their life! They don't get organized because they feel once they start, they won't be able to stop. Indeed, experience bears this out.

A NEVER-ENDING STORY?

How many times have we plunged into organizing, determined to make some headway? We press on doggedly, pushing far beyond our limits into utter exhaustion. When we come up for air, the day's half gone. Or if the phone rings during the session we're subconsciously relieved at the interruption, which we deem of the utmost importance. We shove the stuff into bags or the back room and get out of there. Not only isn't the job done, we've added to the burden. Will organizing ever end?

Consciously Disengaging

Wouldn't it be easier if we could know, deeply in our bones, that we wouldn't be stuck organizing forever? That we could stop whenever we choose and do something else—something we want to do, something we're meant to do. Wouldn't it be easier if when we organize we would make things better, not worse? And that when we leave organizing we could get back to it easily? The Ending Skill helps us do just that. We learn how to leave a situation better than we found it, experience real satisfaction, and have a clear sense of where to go. Organizing doesn't have to be exhausting, or fruitless, or endless. With Ending Skills we can stop gracefully and effectively, whenever we choose.

Pinball Culture

Many of us are in the habit of rushing from one thing to the next with barely a beat between. Like the ball in a pinball machine—boing, boing, zipzipzip, whoosh—we carom from one task to the next and the next and the next, barely present to what's before us. We pack in activities, one backed up into another. The message we hear around us is "More is better; you'll feel great if you accomplish all of this." Well, do we feel great? Hardly. Exhausted is more like it. Do we feel like we've accomplished a lot? Perhaps. More likely we wonder where the day went.

In our culture, many people are not comfortable with endings. Leave-takings are often awkward. Our brief encounters have even briefer closings. We rarely have gracious acknowledgments, warm handshakes, or a satisfied mutual gaze. Most often we uneasily wonder, "What just happened there?" We brush away the discomfort and get on to the next thing.

Grief and Loss

We see cultures that allow long and loud grieving in funerary rites. For most of us, it's embarrassing, unseemly. And we're amazed at how the people of these cultures appear to put the death behind them so easily and go on. Are they callous? Perhaps they can move on so well because they've grieved so well.

Despite Elizabeth Kubler-Ross's work familiarizing us with grief and loss, despite the growth of the hospice movement, despite the endings we encounter every day, we're still uncomfortable with loss. It shows in our difficulty with getting organized. We accumulate stuff and then we cling to it, clutch at it, and don't move it through. We don't let go.

As a culture, we're continually looking forward and oddly, that orientation may keep us stuck in place. We need to look back, close things off, and leave them gracefully so we can move ahead.

A Homeopathic Response

The pin-ball response to endings is to effectively erase any trace of them. They're just too uncomfortable, so we mask our distress with nonstop activity. The soulful response, on the other hand, is to make endings more conscious, rather than blocking them out. We go with, rather than against, the experience. This kind of response is homeopathic: rather than getting rid of our symptoms, we intensify them so that we can work with them more effectively. With Ending we look back at what we've done rather than forward to the next task. We gather up all the loose ends, rather than leave them hanging. We prepare our return to the task, rather than run away from it. And then we disengage from the work, rounding it off for the time being.

ENDING IN ACTION

In order to make our endings more effective, we need to make them more conscious. First we make the boundary between organizing and not organizing clear and then we take specific steps to close the work down.

Define a Time Frame

It helps to consciously define how long we will be at a particular task. The schedule may determine the time frame for us. For example, we might have a free half hour between appointments or an evening hour with no commitments. With good Ending Skills we can do worthy work in whatever time is available.

When there's no externally determined time frame, we set the limit ourselves with the help of our observer. We gather data from the past or from the present situation—how long do we typically work before we "run out of gas"? We make sure our organizing session ends well before that. When we first start out, ten minutes might be all we can do.

See Observing, page 21

We're wise to be kindly and realistic, yet firm when we set a time frame. If we expect ourselves to work for long stretches of time just because the task is so huge, we force ourselves beyond our limit. This doesn't bode well for the future. Who would want to keep doing something so exhausting? We work within our limitations so we don't get frazzled, balky, or discouraged. As we develop the skill, our limits might well expand.

Keep External Demands at Bay

We may find that there's no time at all for organizing. What then? The surrounding culture presses in with messages about all the other things we *must* do besides organizing—things that seem so much more important. Yet, even in the face of such pressure, we can negotiate with the competing parties and put the insistent demands in their proper places. After all, we've already demonstrated that we're willing to put energy into getting organized by reading this book! With Ending Skills in place, at least we can limit the time we do take for getting organized.

With a boundary for the session set, our energy can be contained. We can work freely, intensely, even, within the set time frame. With a good boundary in place we can leave the task cleanly—midstream in a large organizing project, when energy flags, when an interruption comes, or whenever we choose.

Close Down

It takes time to close down. We rarely acknowledge this fact as we zip from one task to another. We forget that whatever we bring into our house will eventually have to be cleaned, repaired, passed on, or discarded. Every activity we consent to implies juggling our schedule to accommodate it. If we don't take the time to end what we start, we'll leave a wide wake behind us as we go. We'd be a lot less frustrated and put-upon if, when we accept a task, we accept it in its entirety, including closing it down. This is what life on earth is about. Things take time.

We do know how to do close-down, and not just in shutting down the computer. Think of how we help a child end her day. We don't just chuck her into bed and leave. We tell the story, tuck her in, kiss her goodnight, and then leave. We do the special rituals that allow us to disengage.

Close-down time isn't tacked on after the end of the session. It happens within it. A quarter to a third of the total time set for the session is generally sufficient for a graceful ending. Say, if the session is set for a half-hour, we stop at twenty minutes and then move into close-down mode. It can help to actually set an alarm so that we don't have to keep track of time while in the session.

Stopping

The challenge is to stop when the time's up. Just stop. Period. We're so used to pressing on—just a few more items, just another little pile, only one more task. Doing "just one more" sets us up for all kinds of difficulties. We find ourselves staying long past quitting time at the office. We're late for appointments. We rush our children. We get sidetracked, sabotaged, and worn out. The trick is to honor our own commitment and stop. Just stop.

The habit of not stopping "until it's done" (whenever that might be), disposes us to do only tasks that fit into the time available. We do the small, easy, time-limited tasks rather than the big, complicated, and perhaps important ones. Sure, we get satisfaction crossing an item off the list, but what kind of satisfaction is it? When we learn how to stop in the middle of a task, we open up the possibility of getting to the complex areas we've been putting off.

Three Close-Down Tasks—Past, Future, Present

The three tasks of Ending relate to the past, the future, and the present. We acknowledge the immediate past—what's just happened in the organizing session—and let it sink in. We make a bridge to the future, identifying what's next so that we can slip into the work easily next time. We gather in the work we've been doing and get back to neutral gear in the present so we can shift out of organizing and into something else.

The immediate past—acknowledge what just happened. The first step is to take stock of what we've accomplished. We use the Acknowledging Skill to notice, for example, that the pile of stuff to sort is visibly smaller. We acknowledge that the floor of the closet is clear by actually stepping in to retrieve clothes. We see the new "parking place" by the door that we've made for the keys.

See Acknowledging, page 29

There may be much more than physical progress to acknowledge. We may have identified a few new categories that will give our stuff a more workable shape. We may have uncovered a task beneath the one we're ending now that will really make a difference. We may notice that working with the bills seems to encourage us, whereas collecting calls to make shuts us down. All of this information supports our organizing efforts.

The value of acknowledgment can't be overestimated. Through acknowledgment we give ourselves the positive reinforcement that impels us to continue. We feel energized, not exhausted.

The future—bridge to the next session. Many people push through to the end of a task because they fear they'll lose their train of thought. In the past when they've stopped midway, it took a lot of time and energy to reconstruct where they were in order to start again. So, rather than stopping when they've had enough, they press on.

If we identify the next task and have it available for the next session, we won't sit before our work and wonder, "'Now, where was I?'" During close-down we name the task that makes a bridge to the future session. For example, we put a "start here" note on the next pile to work on at the desk. We write, "Call Jim to get quote on built-ins" on a sticky-note and post it on our calendar. We put a note on the kitchen cupboard, "Organize pots-and-pans storage next." Identifying the bridge to the next session keeps the energy flowing. Rather than shutting down completely, a thread of the work remains in "active memory" so we can get back to the project easily.

See Sorting,
page 75

See Shedding,
page 111

See Staging
page 85
and Storing
page 97

The present—back to business as usual. The final step in close-down is to get everything back to normal. How often have we run from an organizing project and left everything a mess? We sorted stuff into categories or weeded stuff out, but we didn't close the task down. The sorted papers went back in a pile, and the rejects never made it to the trash. We lost all the good effort we put in.

In the last step of close-down we "park" the current task. We confine the leftovers in some way and move them out of the active working space. Then we can go on to something else. The Staging and Storing Skills offer tools and techniques to appropriately park the work. We gather together everything we've spread out and put it in a neat pile or container. We take what is going elsewhere to its destination (Catchphrase, *Move It On*) and return the space to its business-as-usual state. With everything settled back down, we're free to disengage from the task and do something else.

As we become familiar with Ending, we find ourselves preparing the end as we work. We keep our feelers out for loose ends to gather up. We capture ideas for tasks that bridge to the next session as we go along. A hint of the end might even present itself early on in the session. Music often works this way. Sometimes in the opening moments of a piece, a seed of the end is planted. Then when the actual end occurs, the finish is clear, clean, satisfying, and powerful.

THE GIFTS OF ENDING

The great gift of Ending is being able to stop organizing whenever we choose. We won't have to stay with it forever or until we drop or until we're interrupted (read: rescued). We can disengage from organizing long before we wear out. We can make use of little snatches of time—a half hour or even fifteen minutes. We don't need a full day, or even two uninterrupted hours. We do a little now, a little later. Just knowing that we can stop at will makes it more likely for us to start. Our relationship to organizing lightens up when we know that it won't swallow up our day. The whole enterprise seems less overwhelming and oppressive.

Knowing that we can end gracefully whenever we choose allows us to throw ourselves into the work with gusto. We can bring our whole self to it. In times past we may have approached organizing tentatively, wary of getting swamped.

Partial commitment makes separations, not only in our relationship with the task, but within us as well. On the other hand, when we give ourselves over to a project we foster our own wholeness.

Three-Stage Close-Down

Stage 1. Lay the groundwork for close-down by allotting it sufficient time. Set a boundary for your organizing session. Make sure you aren't expecting more of yourself than you can comfortably accomplish. A half hour might be plenty. Designate one-quarter to one-third of the total time for close-down. Set an alarm not for the end of the entire session but for the transition from active work into close-down mode. Some timers can be set in two stages—the first alarm at the "move to close-down" time, the second for the actual end of the entire session.

Stage 2. Do the work. Setting a timer allows you to throw yourself into the work without having to think about time. Should thoughts outside the session creep in—about what's next, how you're doing, what's left to be done, when and if you're going to stop—set them aside. You'll deal with them at close-down time.

Stage 3. When the alarm goes off, stop. Just stop. There's more where that came from, so you don't have to push through to the end. Begin to gracefully disengage from the session.

Use this sheet to list information from the three stages of close-down:

Stage 1: The immediate past—what just happened? (Be sure to acknowledge collateral accomplishments, not just the obvious ones.)

_____

_____

_____

_____

_____

_____

_____

_____

Stage 2: The future—what's the next step?

_____

_____

_____

_____

_____

_____

_____

_____

_____

Stage 3: The present—what needs to happen to get the scene back to business as usual?

_____

_____

_____

_____

_____

_____

_____

_____

_____

_____

Use this three-stage process to close down any organizing session—when you arrange papers with Sorting, set up your desk with Staging, put stuff in the garage with Storing, or divest yourself of clothes or books with Shedding. The process works for nonorganizing activities as well. Just remember to set a time limit, allot time to close-down, and consciously go through the stages.

Open Ending

When you say, "I'll do it for as long as it takes," you're practicing Open Ending. Beware of the pitfalls of this method:

    putting in a lot of time without getting a lot of results

    working to exhaustion

    having to spend time recovering from the session

    leaving a "wake" to clean up later

If you fall into the pit, you'll have a negative experience that will make organizing less attractive and approachable the next time; so watch out!

You can avoid the pitfalls by (1) coming up for air periodically in a mini-Ending, and (2) preparing in advance for getting back to business as usual.

1. The Mini-Ending

At several points during the open-ended session go through the following steps:

+ Acknowledge what you've done thus far.

+ Strategize what to do next—refocus if you've wandered off task, note your energy level and take a break if necessary, rekindle the flame of whatever motivated you to do the task.

+ Reenter the work.

2. Back to Business as Usual

Either reserve some energy at the end of the open session, or designate a time in the immediate future when you can gather things in, move them along, and get back to normal. It's important to acknowledge the need to put in time at this task. Separating it from the session may help you give it its due.

When you're done with the task be sure to acknowledge your accomplishment thoroughly. Open Ending can be deeply satisfying. Bask in it.

Everyday Beginning

We use Beginning when we

    wash the windows we look out of all the time

    in a research project, read the most important sources first

    when the power goes off, locate the flashlight before checking on any-
    thing else

    prepare the garden soil before planting the seeds

Spiritual Beginning

We use Beginning when we

    identify what kind of volunteer service would both feed
    our soul and help the world most

    decide what will make a difference in our relationship
    with a teenage son and do that

    look at the range of our bad habits and decide which one
    to address now

    choose a spiritual practice that particularly suits us from
    among the many practices available

6. Beginning
Deciding Where to Start

CONSIDERING THE MASS of stuff to be organized, the first question is, where to begin? There's stuff on the dining room table and the kitchen counter, in the basement and the back bedroom, on the desk, the floor, and every available horizontal surface. The task of organizing is as impenetrable as a brick fortress, without doors, windows, or even a chink in the wall. The challenge is to find a way in.

REMEMBRANCE OF SESSIONS PAST

Perhaps in the past, regardless of how overwhelming the project might have seemed, we've taken ourselves in hand and, with great energy, charged the fortress. We started somewhere, anywhere, working with what at least seemed possible to organize—like the LPs in our old record collection or the spices on the shelf. We kept at it for as long as we possibly could before succumbing to exhaustion. Even as we worked, we were distracted by thoughts of everything we didn't organize—like the dining room table or the basement. What an effort! Then, when we went back in a week, or even a day, it looked as if nothing had happened. All those dogged, exhausting hours wasted. How discouraging—to work so long and hard to no apparent effect. And with so much yet to do. Why even begin?

A SIGNIFICANT, POWERFUL DIFFERENCE

Where we begin organizing influences what effect we have and how we feel about it. First, we would be wise to make sure that what we do will make a difference—an undeniable, significant, powerful difference we can see and feel. Then, we would be wise to protect what we do from sinking back into the muck and becoming disorganized all over again. We keep the good work we've done from being compromised by all the work yet to be done. These are the tasks of Beginning: identifying where to start and protecting the progress we make.

How do we ensure our efforts will make a difference? By beginning with a pile or clot or area that we encounter every day. Once we organize it, we'll notice a difference, every single day. Here are some examples:

- ✦ the pile of papers on the chair that we have to move every time we want to sit down

- ✦ the clot of mail on the kitchen counter that we see whenever we walk into the house

- ✦ the complicated, overdue calls that we avoid yet hold in the background of our consciousness

This stuff hangs us up every time we encounter it, which is often. Beginning there will bring immediate, palpable relief.

Is It in the Way?

We identify the areas to begin by asking the question, "Is it in the way?" Stuff can be in the way physically, visually, and emotionally. Here are some examples:

Physically:

- ✦ papers on the dining room table that prevent us from having dinner guests

- ✦ books stacked in front of file cabinets so we can't open the files

- ✦ stuff in the middle of our desk that we have to move in order to work easily

Visually:

- ✦ messes that our eyes land on when we enter an area

- ✦ stuff in our line of sight as we work

- ✦ things that others see as they meet with us

Emotionally:

✦ piles with unfinished business lurking in them

✦ bills we can't pay or charities we're not sure we should contribute to

✦ stuff we hope we'll get to—someday

Call On the Observer

The observer alerts us to what's in the way. With just a tiny part of our consciousness we can note potential beginning places as we go about our daily business. A specific technique from the practice sheets is to tag stuff-in-the-way with "stickies" or colored dots. Whenever we encounter something in the way as we walk, sit, stand, or work, we tag it. Whenever our eyes light upon a mess when we enter a space, we tag it. Whenever we notice ourselves consciously avoiding something, we tag it. There's no criticism involved here, no finger-wagging, no thought, even, of what we're going to have to do with the stuff. We're just reporting—identifying potential beginning places.

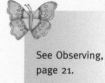

See Observing, page 21.

Stuff-in-the-Way Constricts

Stuff-in-the-way physically limits our movement, constricts our visual field, and cramps our emotional style. When we deal with the stuff, we are free to fully inhabit our space, without the physical, visual, and emotional restraints our stuff had imposed on us.

Not only does the stuff constrict us, it sucks up energy better spent elsewhere. It takes energy to haul the piles of papers to the floor when we want to sit on the chair. It takes energy to put on blinders against the pile of mail. It takes energy to damp down anxieties brought up by the "nasties" pile. Dealing with stuff-in-the-way liberates the energy bound up in it, making that energy available for whatever we choose.

The 80/20 Rule

Even though we're starting with only a small percentage of what needs to be organized, this small part is what will make the most difference. A principle in time management called the *80/20 Rule* states that, in any collection of items, only 20 percent of the stuff accounts for 80 percent of the significance in the whole collection. For example, in our closet, we wear 20 percent of the clothes 80 percent of the time. In a magazine article, only 20 percent of the words carry 80 percent of what we hope to learn by reading the article.

The less significant stuff is not useless—it's just secondary. We need to put it in its proper place—in the background—and bring to the foreground that 20 percent that carries the most significance. Applied to Beginning, the stuff-in-the-way represents the 20 percent that will make 80 percent of the difference once it's dealt with. By exerting only minimal effort, we reap significant benefits.

In contrast, there's a lot of stuff that really doesn't need to be organized—the stuff we can relegate to the background. How much difference would it really make if we organized the files from the person before us in the job, or materials from former interests that we no longer pursue, or old bank statements? Probably not much. Our energy is better spent where we'll really feel the impact, at least at first.

Making a Choice

See Observing,
page 21
and Shedding,
page 111

When there's a lot of stuff-in-the-way, not just a few clots, we need to call on the observer again, to further narrow down where to begin. The observer will tell us what pile *really* is in the way, what horribly messy area we encounter *continually*, what clot brings up the *most* uncomfortable feelings. If we stay with Observing, the outside physical environment and our internal feelings will give us the feedback we need to identify that top-of-the-list beginning area.

FIRM BOUNDARIES

Once we've identified the entry point, we need to protect what we're doing from everything else. We put up a clear boundary around our beginning work to set it off, mentally and emotionally as well as physically. A yellow "Caution—Do Not Cross This Line" tape protects what's being organized from what isn't.

Should attention slip off to tasks yet to do, we reel it back in—gently but firmly. Rather than thinking ahead to the next task, we stay with this one. This is similar to meditation practices where the wandering attention is called back to following the breath. We have, after all, made a valid decision, based on good data provided by our observer, as to where to begin. This information can soothe the part of the mind that calls us elsewhere.

The stuff-yet-to-be-done can grab our emotions, loudly and insistently, or subtly and insidiously. We might feel shame, anger, fear, apathy, or despair at the weight of the whole job. Although we might need to let our emotions have their way with us for a time, we do have a choice. If we stay with what's before us—period—we may be able to bear the emotions that this piece of work evokes, and in so doing, develop our hardiness.

Once the work is done (the Shaping Skills can help with that), we physically protect that island of organization, renewing and repairing the boundary between what's done and what's not as necessary. The hands-on skills of later chapters, especially Staging, give specific techniques for physically protecting our beginning work. Just as important as changing outer habits is countering internal habits of letting thoughts and feelings bleed into what's yet to be done. We respect the boundary and protect our good work as we do it, untainted by what's left to do.

See Shaping Skills, page 69

See Staging, page 85

A Shift of Mind

As we practice calling back attention to the task at hand, a shift of mind takes place. Instead of attending to what's left to do, we attend to what we're doing. We're encouraged to be where we are, rather than where we're going to be or wish we were or think we should be. This awareness is the beginning of change.

BEFORE AND AFTER

Sometimes in order to do the identified beginning task, we need to do other tasks to prepare for it. If, for example, the beginning task deals with papers to be filed, we might note that the file where the papers are headed is stuffed. Before we launch in we need to make room in the file.

The issue is to keep the goal in mind—Beginning. Yes, the filing cabinet might need organizing, and, yes, that might be an appropriate task for another time. For now, however, all we need to do is make it so we can start. Rather than reorganizing the whole filing system, we might simply observe which files are particularly fat and do some shedding there. Thus, in a single, brief session we have what we need to begin—two inches of free space in the file. We're not sidetracked into making the preliminary work into The Work. The beginning task remains uncompromised.

See Shedding, page 111

What Next?

As we finish the designated beginning task, the question arises—what next? We can trust that the next piece of work will present itself in the same manner as the first piece—through asking, Is it in the way? There is no need while working to project ahead. Once the beginning task is taken care of, the next task shows itself. If we continue to ask, is it in the way? we'll continue to have a powerful impact.

See Staging, page 85

As we work, we can note other organizing tasks that come up—like the filing cabinet in the last example. We take a moment to capture that valuable piece of information and collect it with its fellows, maybe in a "to-be-organized" note-catcher. If we would follow every strand of organizing that comes up, we might find ourselves way out on the far edge of organizing, rather than at the central core of the work—the task that makes the most difference.

Instead, as we finish one task, we come up for air, take a look around, and again ask the question. Is this new task that came up as we were doing our beginning task one of the crucial ones that will make a lot of difference? Just because it came up doesn't mean we have to do it. Instead, we can "park" it, and when it's time to begin again, ask the question again. The task that came up during organizing may or may not be next.

Seeding the System

Our efforts might seem insignificant, considering the magnitude of the whole task before us. How easy it is to become discouraged. But consider how every flourishing plant begins. When the little tomato seed comes up, it's certainly modest— only two undistinguished leaves. How easy it would be to say, "Hey! That's nothing" and pull it out. Yet this puny little sprout is, in fact, red, juicy, ripe tomatoes in the making—lasagna, even!

See Acknowledging, page 29

So it is with our organizing efforts. At first they're barely distinguishable. And, some would say, not much to celebrate. However, others would see in those first awkward efforts the seed of a whole system of organization, a whole new way of operating. As we continue to begin and protect our efforts, soon enough we'll feel, undeniably, that something different is happening. Our labor will bear real fruit.

RESISTANCE

For many of us, doing productive, effective organizing is news. We're so used to feeling that our efforts are futile that, when something actually changes, we're taken aback. We don't know what to make of it. For all the distress being disorganized gives us, at least the feelings are familiar. Our feelings of anxiety, fear, apathy, anger, or despair are old friends, in a way. We depend on our disorganization

See Choosing, page 143

for an all-purpose excuse behind which to hide. Embarking on a path of getting organized puts us in uncharted territory. The Choosing exercise can help settle down fears about making real changes.

It takes courage, plain and simple, to step off into the unknown. We haven't a clue what's on the other side (or, perhaps we think we know all too well!). To enter organizing is a brave act. What's curious, of course, is that courage can exist right alongside fear, and indeed, that's how it usually appears. We don't need to get rid of our fear in order to act. It's more a question of choosing which feeling to go with. This time, anyway. We can enter the territory of organizing confidently, identifying a potent entry point and protecting our good work. With Beginning Skills in hand, we know that what we do will make a difference.

Tag It

This practice sheet helps identify a potent place to begin organizing by tagging what's in the way. Work with the sheet over the course of a week or so, as you go about your business.

1. Get some small "sticky notes" or semi-adhesive colored dots that you can remove easily.
2. Pretend you're a stranger who's never seen your space before. Use your Observing Skills *(see page 21)* to look for stuff that's in the way. Be sure to maintain an uninvolved, emotionally neutral attitude. Leave behind any:

   ✦ investment in the outcome

   ✦ history with this stuff

   ✦ judgment about the person who's stuff this is

   ✦ worries about how long organizing the stuff will take

   ✦ concern about where stuff will go

3. Over the course of a week, every time you encounter something that's in the way, tag it. It may be in the way physically, visually, or emotionally.

Physically—

   ✦ taking up prime real estate in the middle of your desk

   ✦ poised to fall off the counter if you're not careful

   ✦ piled in front of a file cabinet so you can't use the cabinet

Visually—

   ✦ what you see when you enter the area

   ✦ in your line of sight as you sit and work

   ✦ what someone else sees as they interact with you

Emotionally—

- ✦ bills you can't pay

- ✦ complicated calls to make

- ✦ difficult decisions

List the tagged piles, clots, or clumps below. Count up the number of stickies or dots for each clump and highlight those with the most dots. The more tags, the more it's in the way. If more than five clumps have the highest number of tags, choose one clump for every five as a priority. You may need to do some after-the-fact Observing to make that call.

You've just identified a potent place to begin, a place that, once you deal with it, using the other skills, will make a significant difference. Congratulations!

Clumps/Clots/Piles	Where Is It	# of Tags	Priority

Sneaking In

The very thought of plunging into the center of organizing where it will make a lot of difference might be too much. You might rather sneak in for a brief moment and beat a quick retreat. Sneaking in by the side door can be easier than making a grand entrance.

Use this practice sheet to identify small, self-contained organizing tasks to do in a single session. These might be rearranging the books on only one shelf or cleaning out the bottom drawer of the desk.

Sneak-in Tasks:

_____

_____

_____

During the course of the obvious, clear-cut task, gather information that might help you approach one of the major, central tasks. You can list this information below. For example, while organizing one bookshelf, you might notice that you need to prepare a distant storage site for books you want to keep for grandchildren, and that some shedding *(See Shedding, page 111)* of college texts might be in order.

Useful Organizing Information:

_____

_____

_____

Be sure to protect whatever work you've done from that yet to be done. Acknowledge *(See Acknowledging, page 29)* that you have made progress and that you've gathered useful information to support you when you choose to continue. Keep the organized spot organized and don't let it sink back into disorganization.

As you gain experience with organizing, you will develop your capacity to bear the changes you make. Soon you'll be able to tackle a central, in-the-way task.

Interlude
Structure in the Surface

MOST PEOPLE'S MOTIVATION for getting organized is that they would like to *do* something rather than be consumed by the details of everyday life. They're bogged down in stuff, distracted, confused, preoccupied, and stuck. They want to break out, do what they're meant to do and not be caught up in all the meaningless concerns that suck up so much time and energy. So, what does it take to do something?

One instinct is to get rid of all the trivial details so we can concentrate on what's important. There is both a kernel of wisdom in that instinct and a danger. Yes, we need to concentrate on what's important. We also need to pay proper attention to the details. The details aren't meaningless, worthless, or trivial; they, in fact, give us access to meaning and power. Music can show us how this works.

Years before becoming an organization consultant, I'd trained as a musician. Music, I know, does something. It might call forth joy or tragedy. It might give a deep sense of satisfaction when everything falls into place. It might feel restless or peaceful. But how? How does everything fall into place? What creates the restlessness or the peace? How does music do what it does? These are questions I dealt with daily as a critic, performer, and scholar.

When an analyst seeks to comprehend how a piece of music works, s/he deals intimately with the notes in the score. Background about the composer may be helpful at times, but in fact, the notes are all that's needed. On first encounter, one note seems like another, more or less. They're all sounds—of particular pitch, timbre, duration, and amplitude, admittedly—but essentially all just sounds. Gradually, however, s/he begins to sense the distinctions between the notes using harmony, timing, and degrees of similarity as clues. Certain notes present themselves as traces of something deeper and more essential operating below the surface, like spring water boiling up from within the earth. These notes connect down through layer after layer to touch the bedrock of the piece. They make the piece do what it does. Although they live on the surface, just like all the other notes, they are more than decoration. They are the source of the structure by which the piece lives and moves.

MACROCOSM IN THE MICROCOSM

Just as the structure of the piece is in the surface notes, and nowhere else, so the meaning and power in our lives is actually in all those seemingly meaningless details that on first glance we deem unimportant. Margaret Starbird in *The Woman with the Alabaster Jar* says, "the material cosmos 'catches the spirit' in her mirror and holds it there, making it visible, as the ocean reflects the wholeness of the sky or the moon the light of the sun."[5] Our personal material cosmos—our stuff—is a means by which we can make spirit, purpose, and meaning visible. Through it we connect with the bedrock of our lives and come to know our true selves. We engage the forces of Nature that are operating within the stars no less than within our stuff.

The so-called trivial details of life have incredible power—the power to make our lives real, or to disappear in smoke; the power to teach us how to embrace ourselves or cut ourselves off; the power to connect us to the grand design or to make our lives ever more trivial. It is precisely through the mundane details that we access the big issues, such as, what is my purpose in life? And how does the universe work? We need look no further.

DISCERNING THE CLUES

How can we distinguish those important details that connect us to bedrock from the trivialities that exist primarily on the surface? In organizing, the process of consciously shaping our environment gives the clues.

See Shaping Skills, page 69

When we first approach organizing, everything seems the same. The mass of papers in the "to be sorted" pile seems to be all just papers. The closet full of clothes to weed out are all just clothes. Yet as we carefully handle each item—using the Shaping Skills of Sorting, Staging, Storing, and Shedding—a pattern emerges. We see that the items are not all the same. Some are connected to our deep longings. Some show who we are, who we've been, and who we'd like to be. Some show what we value and what we don't. This intimate work begins to reveal the connection to bedrock within the surface details of our stuff.

Although we usually rely on reasoning to discern what's important, we would be wise to give our feelings at least as strong a voice in the call. Good discernment engages all our faculties—thought, emotion, body sensation, and intuition. As we handle the papers we sort, we find that a few of them have particular "charge." They may inspire us or intrigue us; they may bring up anxiety or shame. Others are neutral—neither "good" nor "bad." The same with clothing—some pieces delight us, some obligate us (to lose weight!), others are ho-hum. Wherever there's a charge there's a connection to another level. We'd be wise to pay attention.

We may also call on sources beyond our personal responses to discern the clues. Techniques such as meditative prayer, I Ching, dowsing, or casting runes access messages from sources called by many names—universal knowledge, the soul, the Divine, spirit guides, guardian angels, source, the highest *(see Resources: Divination, page 192)*.

The clues often present themselves modestly, subtly, without fanfare. If we're not on alert, we might miss them entirely. Indeed, that's what usually happens in our busy lives. The clues have been there all along, but because they're not loud and insistent, we may not have noticed.

SHAPING OUR STUFF

As we learn to recognize the clues to what's important, our life begins to make some kind of sense. The deeper, generative structures show themselves within the surface details. We experience those "Aha" moments when things fall into place, when they "click." Our purpose in life becomes clearer. The deep water of the artesian well springs to the surface, and we know we're on to something. We've identified what's primary in our life.

The Secondary in Its Place

"So," you might ask, "this primary stuff seems very important; why can't we have just that and dispense with the filler?" Well, life (and music) doesn't work like that. You can't have a piece of music that's only structure. It has to be filled out in time. The little notes (those that come when a piece winds down, when it moves from one theme to another, or relaxes after a big event) support, prepare, and give context to the structural members. It's the details that allow what happens in music to happen. So, in our lives it's the secondary details that give context to the primary concerns of what we are to do.

In music, the secondary details ask for the same level of beauty, technique, and attention as the structural members. The musician doesn't slough them off, but plays them with proper attention to how they fit in, how they support the structure. They're not a burden or unimportant. They are, however, secondary. The integrity, power, and beauty of a piece is in jeopardy when the "little" notes take over and all you hear is diddly details. This is exactly what happens when we get disorganized and overwhelmed, stuck in the morass of details.

On a recent ramble I listened to all the voices in the outdoor choir—several layers of insect drone, a chipping squirrel, call and response of bands of crows, the hum of traffic, an occasional rip of an airplane, and, sadly, chain-saw obbligato. Several of the parts, mostly manmade, are just too loud, too insistent, too stark. Our bigger-better-faster devices easily dominate. Not only are they loud, they don't have the ebb and flow of the natural sounds; they're either on or off. They also lack richness. Electrical devices reinforce the single, stark drone of the sixty-cycle hum (not quite B flat). Now think of the song of a thrush—try to reduce that to one note—impossible!

In our lives it's easy to get caught up in the loud, insistent, stark voices around us and ignore the subtle voices that speak of primary things. When we're in the thick of it, it's difficult to notice what's going on in the larger pattern, much less pay attention to our own voices. Just as when we're singing in a choir it's a challenge to hear the piece as a whole or even hear ourselves sing.

Playing with Balance

Our place is not only in the middle of the choir but also out front as conductor. The conductor listens to the whole and balances all the voices. S/he softens the loud, insistent, stark voices to give them their proper place in the piece. S/he brings out the primary voices. Faithful to the score, s/he allows all the parts to relate to one another harmoniously.

So it is in organizing. Like the conductor, we are active co-creators in shaping the symphony of our life. We bring out the details that connect with what we're meant to do. We tone down the secondary details, not neglecting them, but giving them less energy, urgency, and insistence so they don't mask the important stuff.

It's a matter of restoring balance—shaping, editing, and forming; pulling back from what is too strong and giving weight to what is weak. We play our life in this way, making decisions in service to the template, the master plan, to our purpose in life.

GENERATING POWER

Our aim in getting organized is to move out into the world, to make things happen, to engage our power, and to do what we're meant to. St. Thomas Aquinas talked of three qualities of art, which could apply as well to getting organized. The first quality is *integritas*—the structure as revealed through the surface details in an integrated whole. The second, *consonantia*, is the harmony among all the parts. The third, *claritas*, is the vital radiance that propels the work out into the world. Our aim in getting organized is claritas.

In organizing we discern the structure within the details (integritas) and put them in proper relationship (consonantia). When those qualities are evident in our stuff, claritas, radiance, or power is born. Things happen. We stop struggling against our environment. Rather, we are supported and moved along by it. Those structural patterns that have resided deep inside us become manifest in our stuff. Our thoughts and desires are no longer just private, inner forms. Our stuff is no longer a mass of who-knows-what. Instead, the patterns of our inner and outer environments come into powerful, meaningful relationship. When that happens, we can move out into the world and change it.

Shaping Skills
Intervening in the Physical World

In the beginning, before the Creator intervenes in the Judeo-Christian tradition, whatever there is has no form—it's an undifferentiated mass of stuff. (This might sound familiar as we look at our desk or kitchen table!) Within this mass of stuff, everything—the heavens, the earth, every "thing"—exists. Yet each of these "things" has no independent life. It cannot act on its own. Before divine intervention there is the power of the All, but not yet the power of the Many. The world, with all its "things," is yet unborn.

Naming and Placing—the Act of Creation

The primary act of creation is Shaping. The Creator gathers stuff together, separates one set of stuff from another, and calls each collection of stuff by its name. This is exactly what we do when we exercise the skill of Sorting. The Creator puts stuff in its proper place—the heavens with its lights above, the earth with its creatures below. Similarly, we put stuff in its proper place—the catalogs in a magazine holder, the old clothes stored in a trunk, the rejects in the trash. These are the skills of Staging, Storing, and Shedding.

As we separate and gather, differentiating stuff within the mass, and place stuff where it serves well, we give birth to our world. These deeply powerful acts develop a creative relationship between the personal environment of our thoughts and procedures and the outside environment of our stuff. With our stuff well named and well placed, we can act, like smiths or craftspersons in a beautifully functional workshop, tools at the ready. We have an open space in which to work and play, a channel for our power. We can make use of our talents and do what we are meant to do.

Respectful Intervention

When we intervene in our environment, as we do with the Shaping Skills, it's all too easy to fiddle, meddle, and fix. We just want to get whatever it is organized. Period.

We latch onto ideas that may or may not suit us. Say we hear about arranging recipes by major ingredient and set to it, without attending to how we actually use recipes or how easily they fall into the arrangement. We force our stuff into a preconceived form rather than engaging with it respectfully. Under these conditions, we may feel frustrated, overwhelmed, not fully engaged, and even oppressed. We learn less about ourselves than about how we do or don't fit into other people's systems.

If, instead, we give respectful attention to our stuff, we build our relationship with it and find meaning there. Stuff becomes not a problem to solve, but a teacher that shows us deep truths about ourselves. The patterns latent in our stuff become manifest and give us feedback to respond to. Through this relationship, we can learn something about how we think and operate, perhaps something new. When we respect our stuff, we're more likely to come up with systems that suit us perfectly. These systems work, not just on the surface level, but deeply and widely, with lasting effect.

HERE COMES THE STUFF

Browsing through the health food store we pick up product brochures. We buy the new book we just heard about. A sale flyer mentions the electronic media player we've been wanting, so we get it. The season changes, so we buy clothes. The mail brings catalogs, brochures, and announcements to consider, respond to, file, or toss. Ready access to credit and a wealth of product information make it all too easy to accumulate stuff. Much too much stuff.

What we have reflects not only our taste, but also who we *are*. It's easy to believe that "we are our stuff." We base our identity on the quantity and quality of the stuff we acquire. We feel obligated to have the latest, the best, or what everyone else has. We compare ourselves endlessly to others, linking self-worth to stuff. We pour inordinate amounts of time, energy, and money into stuff.

Acquiring things has become an activity in itself, which suits our commercial culture just fine. Since so much energy is bound up in developing, marketing, producing, and selling stuff, we get caught up in the enterprise and shop just to participate. The acquisition patterns of young maturity—gaining skills, social standing, a family, and, of course, getting lots of stuff—are eagerly promoted by our youth-oriented culture.

Once We Have It, Then What?

Simply acquiring doesn't show the whole picture, however. Once we get the stuff we have to take care of it. We have to place it, clean it, repair it, store it, and, of course, use it. If it's paper, we have to file it, decide about it, pass it on, or toss it. If we don't, we feel the pressure of obligation, or the sadness of unmet commitments, or the distraction of too many desires. Mostly we feel bad. The unread books on our shelves shame us. The unused exercise machine mocks our intention to get in shape. The piles of mail remind us of the obligations we've incurred. All this stuff, which seemed worthy at the time we brought it in, is clogging our environment. We're cramped and crowded, thick with stuff that not only takes up space but energy as well. Where is the breathing space? Where is perspective in such an environment?

The Habit of Desire

We live in an atmosphere of endless desire, created and sustained by our commercial culture. Moses Maimonides in his *Guide for the Perplexed* says, "The soul, when accustomed to superfluous things, acquires a strong habit of desiring things which are neither necessary for the preservation of the individual nor for that of the species. "[6]

Not only our material wealth, but also our commercial culture makes it easy to be caught up in the habit of desire. As John Kenneth Galbraith points out in *The Affluent Society*, it is we ourselves who have fabricated these endless desires through advertising. We then lament the suffering we have set ourselves up for.[7]

These days, many people recognize the futility of endless desire. More stuff is not the answer. Through simplicity circles, books, and programs, many people are identifying their true needs, becoming aware of the influence of advertising, and finding ways to disengage from the habit of desire.

Stuff as Artistic, Spiritual Statement

We can consider the possibility, however, of looking at "I am my stuff" in another light. Our stuff need not only remind us of being in thrall to the production machine, or of being stuck in cultural conditioning. Our stuff can also show forth our best self.

In a very real sense, "I am my stuff" is not a guilty admission but an artistic and spiritual statement. We stand before our stuff as the artist stands before his/her materials. By shaping stuff, we give powerful form to our life just as the potter gives form to clay. By shaping stuff, we reveal our spiritual aspirations in our physical environment. We give our stuff meaning. We decide what we value and see who we are.

SHAPING SPACE SHOWS HOW WE OPERATE

Staging, Storing, and Shedding mirror the particulars of our daily life back to us. The arrangement of our desk is in tune with how we like to operate. The stuff in our closet is stored appropriately, with ready access to the clothing we love and use. What's not relevant to our daily life finds its proper place—out of the active area or gone.

Letting Change Take Hold

Change isn't easy, especially if our body is used to the old way. When we get rid of the big pile of who-knows-what on our desk and replace it with a projects-in-progress holder, we will certainly reach for the old pile a number of times before it sinks into our body that we've made a change. Our muscles are shaped by what we do. Our neural circuitry has certain established tracks. When we change our space, our body needs time to adjust.

The more conscious we are, the better. We can help changes take hold in many ways. Visually, we can note every detail of the new system, every relationship between the project holder and the rest of the immediate environment. Aurally, we can speak out loud, "the active project holder is at my right hand, exactly where I need it, from this moment on," giving our ears something to hold onto. Whenever we use the new system, we can be aware of our hand and arm, consciously experiencing the new body sensations.

Consistency helps too. Every time we finish an active project we "park" it in the project holder. Every time we go to work on it again, we look for it there. In a rush, we might be tempted to leave the active project open on the desk. However, taking thirty seconds to gather it up and park it properly reinforces our decision to use the project holder. Every opportunity to use the new system makes it more and more ours. Once the awkward stage is over, our environment will work with us rather than against us.

Is It Possible?

If we believe the adage, "You can't teach an old dog new tricks," we're in for trouble. First, it's simply not true. We learn new "tricks" all the time. We change jobs and learn a new computer system. We grow older and learn ways to favor achy joints. We adjust to a new neighbor we meet. We deal with parents' aging. The issue isn't that we don't make changes. The issue is that we'd rather not make *this* change.

Resistance is a sign of contact with a level below the surface. Other changes weren't a problem. They might have been merely surface changes or ones that fit into an already existing pattern. Neither make a fundamental difference. When there is a possibility of really shifting things, however, we resist. If we keep in mind that resistance is a sign of contact with meaning and power, we might move through it and see what happens.

See Structure in the Surface, page 63

See Choosing, page 143.

New Information, New Power

When we actually make changes in our environment, we suddenly have a wealth of new information available to us—feedback from "out there" that we couldn't have gotten any other way. Our observer is delighted, busy gathering data of all kinds—how it feels physically to be in this new environment, what our emotional state is like, what thoughts arise in this new situation. All of this data helps us fine-tune our changes, build on them, and take pleasure in them.

As our physical space comes into harmony with our thought processes and procedures, we release the energy that had been tangled up in our disorganized space. We give our environment tender care and embrace more and more of ourselves. We become more effective, more powerful, and at the same time, more loving toward ourselves and our stuff.

SHAPING SKILLS CATCHPHRASES

Active/Archive
Foreground/Background
Here and Now
Like-with-Like
Macro/Micro
Middle Ground
Move It On
Prime Real Estate
80/20 Rule

(See page 181 for definitions.)

Everyday Sorting

We use Sorting when we

> put fruit in one refrigerator bin, vegetables in another
>
> arrange the potluck table so sweets are separated from savories
>
> in a dresser drawer, group socks together, separate from underwear
>
> separate glass, plastic, and metal when recycling

Spiritual Sorting

We use Sorting when we

> recognize that different activities have a similar purpose
>
> identify the patterns in our compulsions, addictions, and habits
>
> arrange a light, bright home altar at springtime; a dark, inward one at winter
>
> bring appropriate people together for gatherings with particular purposes

7. Sorting
Revealing Order within the Chaos

WHEN WE FIRST APPROACH organizing, our stuff can feel like complete and utter chaos—totally disordered. How could we possibly make sense of all this stuff? There are mounds of papers on the kitchen counter, boxes on the back porch full of who-knows-what, closets stuffed to the ceiling. It's endless!

WE'RE ORGANIZED ALREADY; IT'S JUST NOT OBVIOUS

It may be comforting to know that no matter how disorganized our stuff may feel, it's not totally chaotic. In fact, it's already perfectly organized. Right now.

First, it's not endless. There are limits to what we actually do, or even wish to do in the world. No matter how wide-ranging our interests and activities are, we do certain things and not others. We don't have a law practice *and* raise Weimeraner puppies *and* run a conference center *and* drive a taxi *and* run the local homeless shelter (well, maybe we do!). Nonetheless, we go so far and no further.

Second, within those limits there is a unique pattern of how we operate—where our interests lie, what our personal history has been, and how we think about things. There is sense and meaning in it all, but it's hidden. The pattern is just waiting to be revealed.

Revealing the Pattern

Through the skill of Sorting, we reveal the pattern within the jumbled mass. By putting similar things together, we make evident in the physical world the form that's already in the stuff. We untangle the jumble and make categories. We put all the reading together, all the bills, all the telephone calls to make. We gather things together in categories and separate each category from the others. Through this process, the pattern latent in the stuff gradually becomes clear.

Making distinctions, perceiving patterns, and categorizing are particularly human functions. Our brains are hard-wired to do it. For example, at our first encounter with a four-legged furry beast, somebody said, "Dog." From that time on we could look at similar beasts and recognize this one as a member of the class, "Dog." We did it naturally then, and we do it naturally now, all the time. Just because it's natural, doesn't necessarily mean it's easy. Each of us has a different capacity to perceive categories. Some people do it effortlessly; others struggle.

Exactly Enough Structure

Even though classifying and categorizing come naturally, we hate to be pinned down. After all, we are one of a kind, nonpareil, in a class by ourselves. Right? There's no one quite like us and never will be. We refuse to be pigeonholed or put in a box. Our rugged individualist American culture supports, even glorifies, this stance. What we resist for ourselves, we often resist for our stuff. We don't want to constrain or categorize our stuff. We don't want to put it in a box, literally!

Yet, if we don't classify, categorize, and contain, things slip through our fingers. There's nothing to hold on to, nothing to grasp. Either we're awash in a sea of undifferentiated stuff or caught in the exceedingly fine details of each item. Neither works. What we need is exactly enough structure—no more, no less. Yes, we acknowledge the uniqueness of our stuff, *and* we acknowledge that it falls into categories.

In Sorting we find the delicate balance between the one-of-a-kind and the class, between structure and flexibility. I'm reminded of biology class when we looked at amoebas swimming around merrily in swamp water. A chemical was introduced that dissolved their cell walls. Tragedy! The little creatures turned into goo. Another experiment made their semipermeable membranes less porous. Another tragedy. They couldn't grow, eat, or interact.

So we need categories that give our stuff some structure, but not so much that we get stuck in it. Balance is tricky, it comes and goes; it's never stable, always dynamic. As we sort, we get better at finding that balance point between the specific and the general.

ATTENTION AND SORTING

We use our attention in several ways. One is associative, making connections between what's before us and events or ideas from other times and places. The Internet mirrors this way of thinking as we follow links far down a trail. The associative mode is complex, creative, and exciting.

Another way is to pay attention to what's before us in the present moment, here and now. This plodding, simple, firmly rooted way of thinking gets much less respect. In our culture, the associative mode is the more compelling of the two and so is more fully developed. The here-and-now way, because it is less developed, is often awkward and clumsy. We're uncomfortable with it and so use the associative mode whenever possible. In Sorting, that gets us into trouble.

See
The Interplay
of Polarities,
page 119

Pull Back on Associations

We've probably all had an experience like this one. With company coming in a few hours, we figure we have plenty of time to sort through the papers on the dining room table. We begin. There's a magazine and a newspaper—Things to Read. There's a bill to pay, some information on our medication, an invitation, another bill . . . an invitation! Our mind goes off to the invitation. We start reading—a former colleague is getting married next month in Phoenix. Before we know it, we find ourselves reaching for the phone. So, what happened to sorting papers? We're off on an associative junket to the past with our friend, to the future with her wedding, and to Phoenix. Anywhere but here and now.

As we sort, thoughts race through our mind—about what to do next, about decisions to be made, about other times, places, and people associated with what's before us. Associations beyond the here and now pull us off the task of Sorting. Better that we stay grounded in the present moment and call back our attention when it goes off on an association excursion.

Here-and-now attention is very much like a prayer or meditation practice. The idea is to notice when attention slips off the task at hand and, gently yet firmly, call it back. Every time we catch ourselves "elsewhere" and come back to the task, we strengthen here-and-now attention. At the same time, we learn how to disengage appropriately from the habit of associating.

HERE-AND-NOW SORTING

Sorting in the here and now can be a challenge when we first try it. We're wise to start small and proceed with care. We gradually give our stuff shape by gathering and separating it into categories. The Sorting Skill is used with other skills as well, so whatever we learn here can be applied elsewhere.

See Shedding,
page 111,
Staging, page 85,
and Imagining,
page 131

Macrocosm in the Microcosm

The pattern of our stuff is in a small sample as much as it is within the whole mass (*see Catchphrases, page 181:* Holographic Organization *and* Macro/Micro). In order to access the pattern, we need not sort through the whole pile. Thank goodness. The microcosm of a small sample exemplifies the pattern of the macrocosm.

For example, from our pile of unsorted papers, which might be several cubic feet in volume, we pull out an inch or so from the middle, a core sample, if you will. Within that small sample perhaps 50–60 percent of all of our categories will show up. Even though we're only sorting a little bit, that sample will give us most of the categories we'll use in the entire system. The sample seeds the whole.

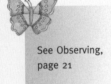

See Observing,
page 21

Identify the Categories

Sorting lets categories emerge through an intimate encounter with our stuff. We carefully handle each item, noting the category name it evokes in us. We listen to what it has to say. We can ask the simple question, "What is this?" and listen to the answer. Internally we do know what this stuff is. The trick is to bring what we know inside out into the open. The observing point of view can help activate our awareness.

When "What is this?" isn't coming forth with a name, other questions we might ask are, "How do I use this?" or "What's going to happen to this?" or "What do I do with this?" These questions might yield categories like, "Networking contacts," "Stuff to give to Harry," or "Craft Project Resources." *(See Resources: Wurman, page 192)*

Cross-Referencing

When an item fits in more than one category, we track down our primary way of accessing the item. We pay close attention when we ask the questions, "How do I think of this? How do I use it? In what context does it come up?" We assign a primary designation based on our answers. For example, health club materials could go either with Medical/Health items such as prescription information and insurance policies or with Personal Interests such as listings of dance venues and information about a hobby. If we think of the health club as more of a Personal Interest than a Medical/Health item we place it with Personal Interests. Then we put a cross-reference note with the Medical/Health items— "for Health Club see Personal Interests." The notation will lead us back to the primary category. If we're still not sure, we might observe ourselves for a while to notice our natural way of thinking about it.

Our Categories or Theirs

Some categories are common since they represent a response to the common culture that surrounds us. Others are utterly unique. We might expect our stuff to fall into generic classifications, like those on the preprinted labels in ready-made filing systems. We look "out there" rather than "in here" for the pattern. Squeezing our stuff into an external structure, however, sets us up for frustration and confusion. Some stuff doesn't seem to fit anywhere. We have trouble remembering what goes with what. Instead of suiting us perfectly, like a tailor-made outfit, the external system, like the off-the-rack item, doesn't quite fit.

If we force our stuff into preconceived categories, our systems become less soulful. We miss an opportunity for a mutually informing relationship between the stuff and our particular way of being. We lose the chance to find deep meaning in our stuff. If, on the other hand, we let the categories bubble up from within, the physical form of our stuff then reflects the unique pattern of how we think and what we do. Our stuff becomes infused with meaning as we build the bridge between what's in our heads and what's in the stuff.

Call It What It Is

When we come upon an item that we can't easily categorize, all too often we delve into it, read it, puzzle over it—all of which gets us into associative mode. We can stay in the here and now by putting it in an "I Don't Know" category, which names what it actually is. The I-Don't-Know pile allows us to keep sorting in the here and now.

We may run into other challenges—an item that's emotionally sticky, something we have to make a decision about, or one that has information from separate categories on the same paper. Instead of getting stuck, we name it and place it in the category that we've just identified—Emotionally Sticky Stuff, Decisions to Make, Stuff to Separate. We call it as it is.

We might find ourselves rummaging through the pile and picking out items in categories we already have in hand. Say we go searching for telephone calls to return. "Search mode" operates more like the associative mode than the "what's-in-front-of-me" here-and-now mode. Although we do end up with a like-with-like pile (which is, after all, what we want), we've only categorized a few items and still have the pile to go through. Better we include everything, addressing each item as it presents itself, and see what it has to reveal.

The Types and Numbers of Categories

Most people's stuff falls into four general categories—task, subject, time, and importance. Each person's mix of categories is unique. Here are some examples.

Task—filing, to read, bills to pay
Subject—XYZ project, gardening, administrative memos, financial
Time—to do today, next week
Importance—priority, to do whenever

A workable number of categories that emerge from a random sample of stuff is six to twenty. With fewer than six, the distinctions may be too gross; with more than twenty, the distinctions may be too fine. Either way is cumbersome. Some categories have significantly more stuff in them than the rest. These ask for a secondary sort.

Sorting as a Creative Act

As the categories that have resided inside us come out, we put our stamp on the physical world. Like Adam, we call these papers "Stuff to be filed," and, poof!, Stuff-to-be-filed comes into existence. What power! It emerges from the amorphous mass and takes on a life of its own. Sorting is, in a very real sense, creating our physical environment. It shapes our stuff in a way that's uniquely ours. Such a creative act is the most human thing we can do.

Capture the Category Names

Once we've identified the category names, we capture them so we won't have to recreate the system every time we sort. Some techniques are: speaking the name out loud, taping the session, enlisting a "sorting buddy" to label the piles as they emerge, or writing the names on sticky-note labels. The practice sheet at the end of the chapter gives a place to list category names.

Let the System Grow

With categories from the small sample in hand, we can pull more material into our category structure. We can take another handful and sort them too. The Threshold Skills identify a good place to continue our work, ensure that we put reasonable limits on our sorting sessions, and help us close down our work so we don't have little piles of stuff all over. Staging and Storing deal with the "fallout" from the sort, making good places for each

See Beginning, page 53 and Ending, page 41

category of stuff to go. Every time we have a sorting session, we will probably find a few new categories and continue to refine our system.

See Staging, page 85 and Storing, page 97

When We Hit the Limit

Good Sorting Skills allow us to change and grow in response to new information. We go along for a while and things make sense—we have a grip on our categories; we see the patterns in our life. Then, somewhere along the way things start getting fuzzy. The categories don't seem to work any more, until we wake up one day utterly confused. I remember this experience when I studied math in school. Just a moment ago things seemed to make sense, but as I approached calculus I crossed a line and became lost.

It's not that all of a sudden we've become stupid. We have, however, hit the limit of the old pattern we've been working with. It just can't accommodate the new information any more. So we go off into the fog where there aren't any patterns.

Rather than try to tack on new categories or patch up the old system, we might start from scratch with Sorting. We step back from our old patterns and take our cues from what's before us. As we sort things out, the fog clears. A new way of thinking emerges, grounded in reality as we actually live it. We make new distinctions and see new patterns. With Sorting we have the flexibility to grow and accommodate whatever changes life presents to us.

Here-and-Now Sorting

1. Begin by identifying some stuff that's in the way. *(See Beginning , page 53 for some help here.)*

   ✦ physically—it may be taking up prime real estate in the middle of your desk

   ✦ visually—it may be the first thing you see when you enter your area

   ✦ emotionally—it may have important things in it that you've been avoiding

2. Lay out the stuff, one item at a time, working from top to bottom. Put similar items together, giving the category a name. Expect uncertainty at first. Before long the items will find their own like-with-like piles.

3. When you're not sure where something should go, put it into the "I Don't Know What to Do with This" pile; you can decide later. Since deciding is an associative function, having an "I Don't Know" pile helps you stay in the here and now and keep sorting.

   Most people have a mix of task, subject, time, and importance categories.

   ✦ task—filing, reading, bills to pay

   ✦ subject—XYZ project, administrative memos, gardening

   ✦ time—today's work, next week, priority

   ✦ importance—priority, to do whenever

An optimum number of categories is six to twenty. If you have fewer, your distinctions may be too gross; if you have more, your distinctions may be too fine. Categories that are significantly larger than the others may need a second-level sort.

List your categories below:

_____

_____

_____

_____

_____

_____

_____

_____

_____

_____

_____

_____

_____

_____

_____

_____

_____

_____

Everyday Staging

We use Staging when we

      fold the laundry on top of the washer, then move it to drawers

      assemble ingredients and tools when cooking a recipe

      put groceries on the kitchen table before moving them
      to the pantry or fridge

      throw trash first in the wastebasket, then take it to the outdoor
      trashcan for pickup

      keep bedtime reading on the nightstand

      set up a baby-changing table with supplies handy

Spiritual Staging

We use Staging when we

      bracket sticky issues and proceed anyway

      move through issues rather than avoid them

      accept ourselves and operate in tune with how we are now

      allow for complexity and richness

      "park" home concerns when we go off to work, and vice versa

8. Staging
Setting Up an Active Area

STAGING SETS UP OUR SPACE so that stuff moves easily through the system. With Staging we beckon stuff along, taking it from the entry point to the next step. Staging makes it easy to start or stop organizing at will so that we can "park" work in progress and get back to it gracefully.

STAGING SHOWS WHAT HAPPENS

Consider this scenario. We walk into the house and start looking through the mail. There's a request from a new charity that we're not going to decide about now. There's a concert announcement; we need to get the kids' schedules before we can consider that. There's a letter from an aging aunt that we'd like to take some time to answer. There's a bill we won't pay until our check comes in. Then the phone rings and it's time to start dinner, so we stack today's mail on top of yesterday's at the back of the counter.

We've just put in some good effort with the mail, but what do we have to show for it? Nothing but a bigger mail pile. The truth of the matter is, we did categorize and consider the mail. However, physically, it appears as if nothing happened. The mail went back to the pile because it had nowhere else to go. With Staging we set up the environment to honor what actually happens by moving it along to the next step.

The Middle Ground

The middle ground between in and out, between the counter and the file, is where much of life takes place. Here decisions are made, information collects, obligations are discharged, communications are sent and received. Without staging areas and tools to honor this complex, active place, stuff gets stuck. It doesn't make it to our filing cabinets, shelves, closets, and containers.

Each category of stuff has its own requirements. Some stuff is on its way to the file; other stuff needs a place to stay while it's on hold. Some stuff needs a decision or a check to be written; other stuff needs to be thrown away. Appropriate tools honor the requirements of each category.

Many of us have anxiety about works in progress. Reminders are everywhere so we don't forget about them. We're preoccupied with what might happen, or is going to happen, or has happened, rather than with what's actually happening now. If we have reliable staging systems, however, we don't have to hold works in progress in our heads. We can temporarily "park" them in such a way that they remind us to do them and it's easy to get back to them.

The "Only Handle It Once" Trap

We might think we shouldn't need tools and systems to accommodate all this stuff-in-transit. After all, shouldn't we "only handle it once?" The reality is—that rarely happens. First of all, we often have to stop in the middle of a task. Even if we have every intention of acting on each piece of mail immediately, our child, colleague, or boss may walk in with a different agenda for us. Good staging systems help manage interruptions gracefully. Should we be interrupted while we're paying bills, we have a place to put them along with their fellows, where they eagerly await our return.

When things get complicated and time presses, we think, "I'll get to it later." And, of course, "later" is just as busy as "now," so a backlog develops. Without appropriate staging tools, we are, in fact, more likely to handle stuff much more than once. If there's no place to put the stuff, it goes back into the pile where it shows up again and again and again.

Much of our stuff—like charities to consider, bills to pay, events to go to, or things to buy—is better dealt with in batches. In fact, it might be wiser *not* to handle them as they come in, but rather let them accumulate. We might pay bills twice a month, or make most charity decisions at year-end. Decisions are often clearer when we group all the options together, rather than deal with them individually, separated by time and space as they arrive. "Only handling it once" may have worked long ago when there was much less stuff to handle. Now, with quantities of stuff in each category, not just an item or two, we need staging tools to give us a place to collect stuff until it's time to deal with it.

Staging in Action

The middle ground between in and out is often the most neglected area in organizing systems. We can shape up this complex area by designating places for stuff to go. We address what to stage, where to stage it, and how.

See Beginning, page 53

See Sorting, page 75

What to Stage?

Prime candidates for Staging are works in progress, things on the way to storage or trash, and the categories of stuff generated by Sorting. Examples of stuff to stage are:

- ✦ incoming stuff, such as mail or flyers we pick up
- ✦ stuff that we can't, won't, or ought not do just now, such as articles to read or a blouse that needs a button sewn on
- ✦ stuff that we're holding on to while a full batch accumulates for the next step, such as ATM receipts or bills to pay
- ✦ stuff that's on hold or pending, such as calls where we've left messages or decisions we need to consult our partner on
- ✦ stuff that's on its way to storage, such as things to file or out-of-season clothes

Where to Stage It?

With stuff in like-with-like categories, we ask, "Now what?" Where does the stuff go from here? Some of it is on its way to storage. Some will be passed on to others—colleagues, family members, or friends. Some we need near us right now. Some of it isn't going anywhere; it's on hold. Once we know where it's headed, we designate areas and tools to help send it on its way.

For example, bills from the mail pile move to the kitchen table, which is where we usually pay them. After the checks are written, the envelopes are headed to the post office, so we might stage them, along with their "out-the-door" fellows, in a basket near the door. The paperwork from the paid bills, on the other hand, ends up in a file. We may place a bin on top of the file where they're staged with other stuff to be filed.

Active/Archive

We place stuff we use frequently nearby and stuff we use rarely farther away. Consider a workspace. Every square inch we can reach from our chair is the "high-rent district," best occupied by stuff we use all the time. Anything else—old papers, doodads, a pen that doesn't work—goes elsewhere.

For example, references we consult all the time, like our phone number card file, are active, but an out-of-town phone book may not be. Similarly, we needn't put every pen we own on our desktop, only those we love and use all the time *(see Catchphrases, page 181:* Like-with-Like *and* Active/Archive). If our current project has reams of backup material, rather than staging it all on our desk, we might put the supporting material on a nearby shelf. As for bills to pay, although we pay them twice a month, we're adding to them whenever the mail comes in, so the bills might well go in the high-rent district.

We create an active work space where everything we need is at our fingertips. This is not to say that the space is sterile. Those inspirational sayings, funny pictures, and photos of loved ones *are* used often. When we clear out the old stuff from the desktop or bulletin board, we'll actually be able to see them. High-rent districts can be anywhere—a meditation corner, a garden, the bedroom, the kitchen.

One of the reasons people feel "strung out" is that, in fact, they are. Their energy and attention spins far out, in many directions. No wonder they feel scattered. Energy is strongest near the physical body, less so farther away. Putting active materials near and less active progressively farther away helps consolidate and focus energy. We bring those things to which we're paying current attention into the foreground and let the rest reside in the background *(see Catchphrases, page 181:* Foreground/Background*)*.

Active Equals Accessible

If it's active, it needs to be accessible. Stuff in the bottom tray of a stacked set is less accessible than stuff in the top tray. On the other hand, the same stuff placed in the slots of a vertical sorter is all equally accessible. Horizontal Staging tends to generate piles, whereas shifting the stuff by 90° to the vertical helps it move along.

In a four-drawer filing cabinet, the second drawer from the top is most accessible, the bottom drawer is least accessible; the front of the drawer is more accessible than the back. So, active files can go in the front of the second file; archive materials can go in the bottom file. The active portion of a particular category can go in the front of the drawer, with the rest in the back of the same drawer.

In small spaces, thinking vertically makes good use of the little space we have. We can hang things on the wall, attach holders to doors, run shelves all the way to the ceiling. The higher up it is, however, the less accessible.

Stage It Where You Use It

We might be inclined to stage things where we think we *should* use them rather than where we actually *do* use them. For example, we might think, "Well, I've got that desk downstairs. Shouldn't I pay bills there?" Although we may be tempted to set up the bill staging area downstairs, we're probably better off going with how we actually work, here and now, rather than how we might work in the future.

Setting up a new bill-paying area may compound our troubles. In order to make the downstairs place workable, we might have to clear out a space, and we certainly will have to change our habits. It may not be worth it. On the other hand, we might decide that, indeed, paying bills at the desk is the better method by far. We're losing bills in the soup; we're horribly oppressed by the thought of bills at breakfast.

Whatever the case, we work *with* the reality, rather than against it. Making our staging tools and areas consonant with how we actually work honors our life as it is lived. We engage the power of the here and now. Perhaps in the future we'll make a change, but for the moment, there are bills to pay, and this is where we pay them.

How to Stage

The tools and areas we use to accommodate work in progress are temporary storage places—parking lots, not the home garage. They provide structures that allow us to leave a task midway and go on to something else. Here are some specific ideas for appropriate staging areas and tools. Not all will be appropriate for every system. We can call on our observer to gather information about which would work for us. The Imagining Skill can also help generate further options.

See Observing, page 21

See Imagining, page 131

+ Filing can park in a bin on top of the file, a slot attached to the side of the file, or in a hanging folder at the front of the file drawer.
+ Stuff to pass on to others might be staged on a chair by the entrance to our office, a bin on the wall near the door, in a pile next to the other person's favorite chair, or in a basket on their door.
+ Stuff we're working on now might be in a vertical file on our desk/countertop, in an accessible file drawer, an open rolling file, or a magazine holder we bring with us wherever we sit down to work.
+ Pending stuff on hold can be in folders in a vertical file on our desktop, clipped together in a special area of the refrigerator, parked in the front of a desk file drawer.

✦ Computer stuff can park next to the computer.

✦ Addresses can collect at the back of the address file.

✦ Bills might assemble in a handy drawer or box, along with stamps and envelopes, for regular bill-paying time.

✦ Reading might go in a number of places—light reading in bathroom or bedroom; work reading, most important on top, on a handy shelf near the desk.

✦ Stuff that requires decisions might go in a folder near the pending stuff or in a central area for consultation with colleagues or family members.

Beautiful, Appropriate Tools

We take into account our personal preferences for materials, style, and color when choosing staging tools. Beautiful, appropriate tools invite us to use them. An oak veneer filing cabinet might be more inviting than the painted metal one we rescued from the trash. We also take into account the physical nature of the stuff: what is an appropriate size and shape for the stuff to be staged? How does it fit into the environment where it's going?

See Imagining, page 131

A cleverly designed wire message holder might be perfect for staging our bills—the right size, shape, and material. On the other hand, gimmicky tools don't always do the job. It's best to take our cues from the stuff, asking it what it wants, rather than fitting it into what the marketplace offers. Imagining Skills can help us come up with attractive tools appropriate to the task. Here are a few more ideas:

a basket near the stairs for items going up and/or down
a bin near the door for items going out and/or coming in
a magazine holder for reading, catalogs, or reference materials
a portable file case with a lid and handle that we can carry with us
an expandable "accordion" file that keeps categories separate
a metal vertical file organizer for current projects, stepped or not
letter trays for specific projects
a handy shelf for frequently used references
cubbyholes or pigeonholes in a desk or shelf
a bulletin board

An Environment That Speaks

When we stage, we arrange our physical environment in harmony with the patterns of how we operate. As our space takes shape, we can witness our patterns taking on a life of their own. We can become familiar with them, listen to what they say, and work with them. Without good staging tools, our patterns are hidden, confused, and inaccessible. But once they're out, we have a new means by which to know ourselves.

Just as paint is the medium for manifesting an artistic idea on canvas, so stuff is the medium for manifesting our life's agenda. The environments we create with Staging explicitly invite, and even require, our participation. Their ingenuity, beauty, and relevance to the chosen task inspires us to use them. For example, we might set up our studio/office so that the computer screen is visible through an open door from the kitchen and living room. Seeing the screen draws us to the computer, inviting our involvement and reminding us of our commitment to pursue computer graphics as a vocation.

With Staging, the papers in our work space and the objects in our home become the instruments by which we make our vision real. Our environment becomes enchanted and full of messages and meaning.

Now What?

Staging accommodates stuff-in-transit from the In-box to the spot where you'll deal with it. Use this practice sheet to identify staging areas and parking lots for your stuff as it makes its way through your system. The question for Staging is "Now what?" Now that you have it, what should you do with it? How to best set up the space to move things along.

Be sure to make use of the Threshold Skills to decide where to start and close the work down when you're finished.

What
Use the categories generated by a Sort or use the Beginning Skill to find a small sample of categories to start with.

Where
Determine what is Active and what is Archive (*see Catchphrases, page 181,* Active/Archive). Things used frequently should be staged closed at hand; things used, added to, or consulted less often should be farther away. Protect the high-rent district—the area immediately at hand when you process stuff. Active stuff should be there. Look to the Storing chapter for help with archival stuff.

Move things in the direction they're going (*see Catchphrases, page 181:* Move It On). If it's going out the door, stage it near the door; if it's going in the file, stage it on top of, beside, or inside the file.

How
Make sure your tools and areas are inviting. Pay attention to your preferences for color and material while at the same time honoring the physical requirements of the stuff. Make your areas both beautiful and useful.

What	**Where**	**How**			
Category of Stuff			Active/Archive?	Move It On	Tool/Area

Areas and Tools for Specific Tasks

You can work through common staging questions here. Go with your current way of operating as much as possible. Gather similar things and tasks together; keep different things, or things that you deal with in different places, separate. Take time to observe before designating tools and areas so that you come up with inviting tools placed according to the catchphrases *Active/Archive* and *Move It On*.

Mail-Handling

Where does mail come in? _____

Where do I sort mail? _____

Where does the "fall out" go?

    Catalogs—where do I look at them? _____

    Reading—where do I read? _____

    Decisions—where do I make them? _____

    Events—where does the information collect? _____

    Other _____

    _____

Bill-Paying

Where do I pay bills? _____

Where does paid bill paperwork go? _____

Where do the outgoing paid bills go? _____

To-Do Spot

What are the categories of to-dos and where are they best placed?

Calls to make _____

Letters to write _____

Errands to run _____

Other _____

_____

Decision Spot

Where do I make decisions?

what to buy _____

what events to attend _____

the importance of to-dos _____

identifying I Don't Know items _____

Other _____

_____

Pending Projects Parking Place

Where do I park pending projects?

Items on hold _____

Waiting for a response _____

Works in progress _____

Everyday Storing

We use Storing when we

>   put coins and maps in the car
>
>   keep credit cards in our wallet
>
>   shift seasonal items—clothes, equipment, decorations
>
>   put frozen food in the freezer

Spiritual Storing

We use Storing when we

>   keep mementos of examples of strength, inspiration,
>   and connection to draw upon in hard times
>
>   put aside attention to old habits that we've already transmuted
>   from "bad" to "good"
>
>   keep certain relationships in the background of our consciousness
>
>   move old ways of thinking out of the way
>
>   revisit journals to refresh our current way of being

9. Storing
Setting Up Archives and Resource Collections

ARCHIVES AND COLLECTIONS show where we've come from and where we're going. They let us sense, tangibly, how rich and complex our lives are. Our archives are evocative; they hold memories both sweet and bitter. Our resource collections hold promise for a future both exciting and daunting.

THE TREASURE TROVE

Over the course of our lives, we assemble a treasure trove of stuff. The attic, the trunk, and the box are repositories where, on a rainy Sunday, we physically touch our past in photos, birth certificates, bank statements, old class notes, concert programs, or books we've read.

We also assemble collections to support our pursuits now and into the future—reference books, telephone directories, tools, off-season clothes, special toys to pass down to the next generation. As our interests evolve, our resource collections similarly evolve.

STORING IN ACTION

Our storing systems mirror how we think, how we operate, what our history has been, and what's important to us. Storing involves looking at what we store, where we store it, and how we store it.

What to Store
Major classes of stuff to store are:

+ legal documents—birth certificates, tax records, passports, and records such as paid bills, financial statements, or medical records
+ resource materials—clipping files, address books, manuals, cookbooks,

and tools such as books, clothing, kitchen ware, or bathroom supplies

✦ personal collections—coins, Barbie dolls, beautiful stones, soil samples, and memorabilia such as journals, photos, toys, or notes

Legal Documents

The largest body of material we're legally required to keep are tax records. Even professionals have widely varying recommendations about how long to retain them, and, for that matter, what constitutes a complete record. The minimalists say three years of returns plus their backup materials—cancelled checks and bills for deducted expenses, and records concerning assets such as real property or investments. Others say seven years; still others say we need to keep them all. If the return is simple, fewer records are needed; if it's complex, more is required. In the absence of hard-and-fast rules, we base our decisions on the advice of professionals we consult and on our comfort level.

Other documents to keep are birth certificates; marriage and divorce documents; citizenship papers; passports; wills; powers of attorney; financial documents such as insurance policies and stock certificates; and copies of contracts into which we enter, such as rental agreements and promissory notes. Beyond tax records and personal documents, everything else we keep is discretionary.

For example, we may decide to keep copies of medical test results if our health history is complex and of importance to us. We might retain utility bills while we have electric heat, knowing that we will want to compare them after we make a planned conversion to gas. We might keep only a year or two of bank statements if we find our bank trustworthy. There are no hard-and-fast rules here either. Except for the legal documents, what we keep for administrative records is up to us.

Resource Materials

We draw on resource materials now and in the future—clothing, both in season and out, everyday and special occasion; references that we consult; tools and supplies we use; information about our interests and activities. Considering the wealth of information and stuff available to us, the resource collection can be huge.

As we assemble materials to store, we take a fresh look at who we are. We might find a whole set of recipes from a "former life" when we baked with white sugar and flour, which we no longer use. We might find masses of clippings for decorating ideas that no longer inspire us.

Storing often brings up occasions for Shedding. Letting go of stale stuff from old interests that no longer engage us can be liberating. It can also be painful. We're wise to be gentle with ourselves as we grieve what is no longer, and even more poignant, grieve what will never be.

See Shedding, page 111

Personal Collections

We see history in our stuff. College notes recall those golden days, old birthday cards remind us of friends long gone, stones and feathers evoke seashore holidays. Our personal collections are rich storehouses of who we have been and who we are; they are precious and filled with meaning.

Yet our collections, by their sheer volume, may also be overwhelming and oppressive. In the past, entire family histories might reside in one attic, or even one trunk, perhaps even in one small piece of jewelry passed down from grandmother to granddaughter. Nowadays, many of us have boxes and boxes of personal stuff. Is it because of our uncertain future? Or that families are so dispersed? Or our materialism? Or avoiding the present by desperate clinging to the past? Whatever the reason, we're often weighed down by our personal collections rather than enriched by them.

The issue comes up strongly when we move. Shall we, once again, pack up all those heavy boxes of college notes? Or shall we keep just those from the professors we loved. If space isn't an issue, we may keep all the stuff. Nonetheless, it does take energy to set up a storage place for it.

Where to Store It

We devise storage systems based on how accessible we would like the stuff to be. The materials we work with, add to, and refer to regularly as we operate every day are best stored near us. For example, we might store the pots we cook with all the time in the cabinet nearest the stove. We store in-season clothes that we love in our line of sight as we open the closet. We store current bank statements in the front of the file drawer. The Staging chapter *(see page 85)* gives ideas on where and how to store such active materials.

Other stuff is less active—the references we consult only occasionally, the magazines we've read, backup materials for projects in the works. This stuff can be near, but not in the most accessible place. For example, the less frequently used pots can be deep in the back of the cabinet, high on top, or in a low pantry drawer. Clothes we wear occasionally can be at the far end of the closet. Last year's bank statements can be in the back of the file drawer.

We're wise to group similar things together within each area. In the kitchen, we store all the tomato paste together (then we'll know how much we have), along with the sauce and pasta. In a clipping resource file, we group subjects together, like "personal growth," "travel," or "investments." In the basement, we put skis and poles together.

The Distant Archive

Material that is over and done with can move even farther away. When storing things out of the immediate area, it's wise to make it easy to retrieve the material should we ever need it. We can label the box with a general contents statement, where the material came from, and the date archived (e.g., "Taxes 1990–95 from lower left desk drawer 4/15/02")—enough information to trigger our memory.

Then we make a notation on our "key to the archive" of what went where when (e.g., "Taxes 1990–95 to south end of attic 4/15/02"). The "key to the archive" can reside in an active place, say, inside our first file drawer, so that we can know what's where without having to hunt around for it or dredge up the location from memory.

Having a key to the distant archive settles down "out-of-sight/out-of-mind" anxiety. We can confidently use those out-of-the-way storage places without worrying that we won't be able to find something should we need it. These principles apply to everything we need to store, not just paper—clothing, books, kitchen equipment, memorabilia, tools, or infrequently consulted references.

Important Documents

Where we keep important documents can range from a dresser drawer to a safe deposit box, based on our level of comfort and security. Wherever we keep them, we're wise to leave a trail in some readily accessible place should someone else need access when we're not around. We can list the location of important papers in an envelope in the middle desk drawer, the back of the file cabinet, a top dresser drawer, or in our address book, and let our nearest and dearest know where to find them.

Files

Considering the volume of paper that most of us store, file boxes, drawers, or cabinets are often the most appropriate tools to accommodate them. Here are specific strategies for filing systems. These principles can be applied to other storage systems as well.

To alphabetize or not. The alphabet doesn't always serve well in setting up a file. Such a system may have "auto insurance," "banking," "car repair," and "financial planning"—A, B, C, F. This may work for a while, but as the system grows, remembering what we called something becomes more and more difficult.

Better that we arrange files according to how we think about them and how we use them. If we group all the financial/money stuff together, when we think "money" we only have to look in one place. The physical arrangement reinforces how we think, and how we think appears in the arrangement. Such an arrangement feels natural, intuitive, and personal. It reflects our own individuality back to us, rather than some generic, pre-existing form. The Sorting Skill can help us come up with appropriate groupings.

See Sorting,
page 75

There are cases where alphabetical arrangement may work best. For instance, client files might be arranged alphabetically by last name. Within the "financial" area, each entity might be filed alphabetically—*B*ank of Anytown, *E*quity Mutual Fund, *W*orkers' Credit Union (B, E, W).

Particular filing challenges can be solved by the alphabet. In a personal reference library of journal articles, functional organizing by topic may not be possible if the subjects interconnect and overlap. Even filing by author might present a problem, since one author might be principal author in one article and second author in another. In this case, the solution might be to arrange the article strictly by title and make a cross-reference key to the author.

Cross-Referencing. When we think of an item in two ways, we need to leave a trail so that if we are in one location we'll be guided to the other. With such a challenge, we might call in our observer to notice how we think of our stuff most often. We observe that we refer to a paper by title, and occasionally by author. We then file them by title and leave a cross-reference in the spot where the author's name would appear that leads us back to the title. Under "Schmoe, Joe" there's a reference that says "see 'Feng Shui for the Home'."

See Observing,
page 21

The physical reinforces the conceptual.
Nesting: One way to set up a file is to use "box-bottom" hanging files for the larger categories and, within the box-bottom, use manila folders, with all the tabs on the same side. This set up visually reinforces like-with-like. Folders within a large category may be the same color as well.

Active/Archive within a file: Often we clog up active file space with all kinds of old stuff, thinking we should put like things together. Instead, within a file drawer, we can make the active stuff more accessible by using the moveable divider. We put archive material behind the divider and active stuff in front— bills to be paid in front of the divider and paid bills behind.

Chronological consistency: When adding to a file it helps if we put the new material consistently either in the front or the back of the file—either will work as long as it's consistent. Thus the file is automatically sorted by chronology. Should we decide to shed some of the stuff or move it to distant archive, we know that all the old stuff is in the back (or the front).

See Shedding, page 111

See Imagining, page 131

How to Store

What we use for storage needs to be appropriate to the task—a good size and shape, and sturdy enough to do the job. We can go vertical by using shelves that go all the way to the ceiling. We can stack boxes if we label the sides as well as the tops. Whenever possible, we group items according to like-with-like—all the old financial statements and tax returns in one corner of the attic, all the family memorabilia in the other corner. Here are a few ideas for storage tools. A session of Imagining can come up lots more.

- ✦ file cabinets on the other side of the room; back half of a file drawer; bottom drawer of a two- or four-file cabinet
- ✦ transfer cases, bankers boxes, storage bins made of plastic, cardboard
- ✦ shelving, boxes, trunks, lockers, etc. in other rooms, garage, basement, attic

KNOTTY STORING ISSUES

Storing can bring up the issue of what we really use. Within our resource collections—magazine clippings, clothes, books, gadgets, sports equipment—what are indeed useful resources for our present life, and what are merely interesting ideas, possibilities, or even pipe dreams? Do we want to be surrounded by possibilities? That might seem exciting and encouraging; on the other hand, it might be discouraging and depressing.

Every time we look at the political articles, we may feel shame at not having written the letter to the editor. Every time we come upon the craft materials, we feel obligated to make the project. Every time we see the ski stuff, we feel the urgency to use it, even though we're no longer really interested in skiing.

We can observe these feelings and acknowledge the reality they represent—that skiing no longer holds the charge it once had; that the political issue is still important; that handwork is vital to our engagement with the physical world. Once we acknowledge the reality we can act accordingly. We pass on the ski equipment rather than storing it. We draft the letter. We take up a craft project more in line with what suits us. Storing gives us another opportunity to learn about ourselves and find meaning in our stuff.

Storing Practice Sheets

The following practice sheets take you through the storing process for the different categories of items—legal documents, resource materials, and collections. The process for all categories is as follows:

Identify What to Store
If you don't know already, identify stuff for storage. Move through your space and tag likely items to store such as (1) stuff you don't use that's taking up space in the active area, (2) similar stuff that's scattered around in different locations, or (3) stuff that's over and done with.

Gather Like-with-Like
Begin the process by gathering similar material together. Say, you want to set up storage for bank statements. Go through the entire space to gather together all the statements in one place so you know how much stuff you will be storing and what containers would be appropriate. Gathering like-with-like can trigger a Shedding session. Say, you decide to keep only a few years of statements. Look to the Shedding chapter *(see page 111)* for hints on how to weed out the material.

Note Retrieval Triggers
Think of how you want to retrieve the stuff: in what situations will you need it, and how often would you go to it? If you use it frequently, you'll want it near you. If it's history, it can be farther away. How do you think of it: by subject area, by the time of year when it's needed, by the personal relationship that's embodied in the stuff? The Staging chapter *(page, 85)* can help here.

Set Up the Storage Location, Put in Containers,
Label, Move, and Track
With information in hand about (1) how much stuff you're storing and (2) where it would go based on frequency of use, designate an appropriate storage location and container. Be sure your containers are adequate, appropriate, and inviting. Then, do the work: box the stuff or set up the file. If need be, label the container with its contents, where the material came from, and the date stored (e.g., "Taxes 1990–95 from lower left desk drawer 4/15/02"). Move it to its storage location. Leave a trail in a

handy "key to the archive" of what went where when (e.g., "Taxes 1990–95 to south end of attic 4/15/02") for distant storage.

Legal Documents and Records

Identify & Gather	Retrieval Triggers	Storage Location/Tool	Label & Track

Legal Documents

    Birth certificates _____

    Tax records _____

    Passports _____

    Other _____

Records

  Financial

    Bank _____

    Bank _____

    Other financial _____

  Medical

    Insurance policies _____

    Medical records _____

    By family member _____

    Other _____

Resource Materials—

Such as addresses, clippings, tools, books, product information, etc.

Identify & Gather	Retrieval Triggers	Storage Location/Tool	Label & Track

Personal Collections—

Such as memorabilia, photos, notes, coins, etc.

Identify & Gather	Retrieval Triggers	Storage Location/Tool	Label & Track

Key to the Distant Archive

When you move materials out of the immediate area, use this sheet to list where the material went. You can then consult this sheet to locate archived material easily. Noting the former location and the date archived can jog your memory.

   With this information readily accessible you don't have to worry about where things are or hold the information in your head.

General Description of Contents	Former Location	Date Archived	Archive Location

Everyday Shedding

We use Shedding when we

 clean out the refrigerator

 decide which social invitations to accept, which to refuse

 decline getting some items at the checkout when we shop

 determine how to spend the money in our pockets while on vacation

Spiritual Shedding

We use Shedding when we

 reject a job offer

 stop a spiritual practice that no longer serves

 end a relationship for the good of all concerned

 let go of "scripts" that keep us insulated from the flow of life

IO. Shedding

Identifying What We Don't Need
and Moving It Out

IN AMERICA TODAY it's all too easy to acquire stuff, lots of stuff. There's stuff coming in all the time—newspapers and magazines, mail, brochures, flyers, books, gadgets, and clothing. Even with excellent recycling programs, charities to accept castoffs, and solid waste systems, we don't let stuff go nearly as effortlessly as we take it in. We keep far more than we need.

Physics tells us that if we don't let things go as we bring new things in, the system backs up. Clogs, clots, and clumps of stuck stuff gum up the works. Stuff constricts us, drains our energy, confuses us, and makes our path through life unclear.

EASY COME, NOT SO EASY GO

Although we might long to shed stuff, actually getting rid of it brings up complicated issues, among them loss and grieving, confronting our life purpose, belonging, and clarifying our values. No wonder we have trouble shedding.

- ✦ We come face-to-face with loss. In a culture that's uncomfortable with grieving, most of us avoid loss whenever possible; we're unskilled and unsupported in dealing with it.
- ✦ Having lots of stuff gives us an endless list of things to do. We spend so much time acquiring, maintaining, and using stuff that we don't have time to consider what our life is really about.
- ✦ Stuff gives a sense of participation in the culture; without it we feel disconnected. Stuff gives us a sense of power and wealth; without it we feel impoverished. Stuff gives us a sense of identity; who are we if not consumers?
- ✦ Shedding exposes our values. When we keep what's important and let go

of what isn't, everyone can see what our values are. They're no longer hidden in a thick fog of stuff but out in the open for all to see.

Shedding is delicate business indeed. It calls forth courage to come out of hiding. It calls forth a deep sense of self. It engages us with the surrounding culture as a whole person rather than primarily as a consumer. It teaches us to bear loss with dignity. Shedding is powerful as well as delicate.

SHEDDING IN ACTION

See Beginning, page 53

See Ending, page 41

We can head off becoming overwhelmed in Shedding by wise use of the Threshold Skills. The Beginning Skill helps us find a place to start where we will get tangible results. The Ending Skill helps us set reasonable limits so we don't get exhausted or overwhelmed. We'll feel accomplishment and leave the scene better than we found it.

Pin Down Criteria with a Small Sample

Anybody can make a case for keeping just about anything—it has potential, we might use it someday, somebody might need it, and on and on. When we try to decide about each item on its own, the criteria constantly shift. Every item seems so important. We can short-circuit this decision dilemma by setting some criteria first, using a small, manageable sample.

Within the body of the stuff to be shed we pull out five items at random—five books to be shed or read, five pieces of clothing to be kept or passed on to charity, five clippings to file or toss. This small sample seeds the entire process.

From Yes to No

We lay out these few items so we can see them all at once. Within the sample it's usually possible to identify one that's more attractive than the others—one we know we'd like to keep, one that has a positive charge for us. We then begin a physical arrangement that reflects the attraction. We put the thing to keep to our dominant-hand side—on the right for right-handed folks, on the left for lefties. This is the Yes side.

Within the remaining items it's also usually possible to identify one we don't want as much, one we're willing to toss, one that doesn't attract us. We put that to the other side, the No side. We've now defined the poles of a range—from "Yes I want to keep this" to "No I can toss this."

The next step is to compare each of the remaining items to the boundary poles. We may encounter one that we want even more, or even less. That item then becomes the outside delineator. One by one we compare and place each of the items from the sample along the continuum.

Right from the beginning our work has shape; we have something to compare each item to. With our preferences and attractions out in front of us, reasonable criteria begin to emerge. We can then pull other items into the continuum, comparing and placing each item.

What emerges is a percentage distribution of roughly 20 percent-60 percent-20 percent—the 20 percent we know we want to shed, the 20 percent we know we want to keep, and the 60 percent we're not quite sure about. The Yeses show what we value; the Noes show what we don't. The bulk of the stuff falls in the Maybe category.

Clarify the Criteria

Before we do Shedding, we know, but only in an unformed, nonspecific way, what our criteria are. As we shed, our preferences stand out in relief. We see our history, the way we operate, the obligations we've accepted, and our future plans mirrored back to us. The touchstones by which we decide what to toss and what to keep become ever clearer. The shedding process brings our criteria out into the open and gives our stuff meaning.

Capture the Criteria and Move Out the Noes

As we shed, we capture the criteria so we don't have to recreate them every time we work. Before throwing away the Noes, we ask, "What is it about this that allows me to confidently let it go?" Some answers might be:

It's out of date, expired, over with, or no longer applies.

I'm not interested in that kind of thing anymore.

It's not important because . . .

I don't need more than one.

I don't need all the supporting material (ATM slips, credit card receipts, etc.) now that I have the consolidated statement.

I want all the memorabilia to fit in the trunk; I have limited space.

It doesn't fit, it's the wrong color, it's broken.

I don't like it because . . .

I thought I would be doing that, but I see now that I won't because . . .

Once we've captured the criteria, we move out the Noes as soon as possible so we don't create another clog at the exit point. Rather than puzzling over the perfect place to recycle them or pass them on, we might just have to put them out on the street—this time, anyway. Between now and the next session, we can identify places to accept castoffs and build that process into the next session. For now, we need to sense that we're making headway.

See Staging,
page 85
and
Storing, page 97

Integrate the Yeses

Next, we pay good attention to the stuff we're keeping. This is the stuff that's made it through the cut. We've looked at it, handled it, and decided that, by golly, it stays! We honor its survival by putting it in the most appropriate place. Staging and Storing Skills can help here. We capture the criteria for the Yeses as well. Some of these may be:

an event that's coming up
information on a new, promising interest
materials for an upcoming job search
memento from dear Bertie, who's gone now
I like this author; this is her best work
the consolidated statement
the current year's records

Isolate the Maybes

Most of the stuff is in the Maybe category. If at all possible, it's wise not to force the decision about the Maybes before we are able to or before we need to. At first our shedding criteria are not quite formed. They're still soft, like the shell of a "shedder" lobster. In the beginning we, like the lobster, are particularly vulnerable. We're only just learning how to shed. We may never have thought so specifically about what we value.

Instead of forcing the decision, we isolate the Maybes in a box or bag, labeled with a general description of the contents so we can retrieve it should we need to. We date the label so we'll have a sense of its "age." Then we move it out of the way to a less active space—the back bedroom, a little-used hallway, behind a piece of furniture, or masked with an attractive screen. After it's sufficiently "matured"—which may be days, weeks, months, or years—we revisit it. When the time comes to deal with the "matured" stuff, the decisions may fall into place. Our criteria may be clearer. We may have developed our capacity to grieve and so can let go more comfortably. If we wait, shedding the Maybes may be considerably easier.

Back into Circulation

Shedding can be particularly satisfying when we put stuff back into circulation. We pass it on to someone who really needs it. We donate clothes, back issues of quality magazines, books, or household items to a charity thrift shop, elderly housing, or a shelter. We recycle paper. We have a swap for our friends to exchange trash for treasures.

Each community has its own instruments for recirculating stuff. Some organizations come to us and happily cart off our rejects, no matter how few or how many there are. We'd be wise to investigate the possibilities by asking around, making calls, looking in the telephone directory, keeping our eyes and ears open, and doing some Imagining either alone or with friends or family. The next time we do Shedding, there will be an acceptor mechanism in place for our castoffs.

See Imagining, page 131

To Shed or Not

With criteria in hand, we can assess each item that comes seeking entry into our lives, and let it in or not. In old Robin Hood movies there was a great, thick door to the castle with a sliding peephole. Whoever wanted entry would rap on the door. The peephole would slide open and a huge, fierce eye would look out. The person would state their business, and the burly guard, on orders from the king, would bid them enter, or not.

It's the same with stuff that comes to us. When one of those "No" items comes knocking, the faithful sentry at the door turns it away. For example, if our shedding practice has shown us that we're no longer interested in a particular style of healing, we know now that we don't have to pick up announcements for those workshops anymore. We don't let it in. Then, miracle of miracles, we won't ever have to shed it!

With good criteria in hand, we have a say about what we bring into the system from this moment on. Of course, a lot of stuff comes in unbidden. We're on mailing lists; we get catalogs. Still, we can telephone, write, or email to get off the lists *(see Resources, p. 192)*. Once we clarify what we really do want, we pull the weeds and let the flowers bloom.

What Do I Need?

There is surprisingly little that we're legally required to keep—mostly personal documents and tax returns. What we do keep is largely discretionary. In our thing-oriented culture, many people rely on their stuff to provide

See Storing, page 97

them with security and comfort. As we shed, however, we find that what remains has proportionately more significance. We can feel secure with only one bottle of glue, not three. We can have access to information via our library card, not by a personal magazine collection. It's like boiling down gallons of sap to make maple syrup. We have less, but what we have is more concentrated.

On the other hand, if we have plenty of space and we're not crowded out or bothered by our stuff, we might be better off storing it as it is, without shedding. We might just get our old college notes and childhood stuffed animals out of the way and carry on. The Storing chapter *(see page 97)* can offer good ideas and strategies.

Shedding can be valuable in itself, whether we need it or not. We all know the tender, bittersweet nostalgia that comes from going through old papers, old clothes, old children's toys. Shedding brings us in touch with the past.

Shedding gives us an encounter with our sense of what's important. We refresh our notion of who we are, who we have been, and who we would like to become. Shedding helps us rely on the resources within us rather than the stuff surrounding us. We claim our power, let go of stuff, and still remain ourselves. We gain peace of mind, confidence in our choices, and clarity, not to mention the clear space where all that stuff used to be. As in refining metal, we melt away the dross and are left with only the gold.

Yes/No/Maybe

1. Take a small sample—about five or six items—from your stuff to shed. Lay them out so you can see each one.

2. Identify one item in the sample that you'd most likely keep; put that on your right. Identify one item that you'd most likely throw away; put that on your left. You have now defined the poles of the what-to-keep/what-to-toss scale. (Switch right/left for left-handed folks.)

3. Compare each remaining item, one at a time, to those at the poles, arranging them, right to left, within the scale. There may be some you clearly want to keep, others you clearly want to toss, and several that fall somewhere in the middle.

4. For the items at the poles, ask yourself: What about this item makes me want to toss it? What about this item makes me want to keep it? Through this process the criteria for your decisions become clear. Toss criteria could be: *out of date, wrong color, broken, I'll never do that, I only need one of these.* Keep criteria could be: *a memento of dear Tom, tax record, I'll do it this year.* There is no "right" way to do this. The question is not what you *should* toss, but what you *would* toss. Each person's criteria are unique; none are "better" than others. List your criteria below:

Criteria for tossing:

_____

_____

_____

_____

_____

_____

Criteria for keeping:

_____

_____

_____

_____

_____

_____

_____

5. Bring other items into your sample scale, comparing as you go. Take as much or as little time as you choose (see Beginning, page 53 and Ending, page 41 for help). Most people end up with 20 percent to keep (Yes), 20 percent to toss (No) and 60 percent in the middle (Maybe).

6. Get rid of all the "No" items.

7. Put the "Yes" items in the very best place (see Staging, page 85 and Storing, page 97 for help).

8. Put the "Maybe" items in rough storage (the back bedroom, attic, etc.), labeled with the date processed and a general description (e.g., "5/7/01— College Notes Maybes"), and let them age for a while. After time has passed and your criteria are clearer, it will be easier to decide.

Interlude
The Interplay of Polarities

HUMANS IN THEIR UPRIGHT STANCE form a bridge between earth and sky. How simple this seems, how obvious, how self-evident. Our head is in the air; our feet are on the ground. Of course. This physical fact embodies the great challenge of humanity across all ages, cultures and conditions—to exist in not just one realm, but two, simultaneously. Yes, we are like the animals, and, yes, we are like the angels. We live where earth and sky meet—a *both/and*, rather than *either/or* species.

THE PLACE BETWEEN

Our form reminds us of our calling—to withstand, work with, and embrace paradox. We acknowledge both light and dark, movement and stillness, the spiritual and the mundane. Our challenge is to stand between the polar opposites and hold the tension gracefully.

At the midpoint between the poles, the entire, 360° range of possibilities is accessible. We are in the moment, creative, and ready for anything, like the dancer whose strong, supple body responds freely to the muse. To take up the midpoint position, we need to be aware of the polarity continuum and where we are along it. Then we can adjust and choose.

Our personal history and the culture in which we live influence where we stand and how aware we are. We have deep grooves in our behavior that dispose us to do things in a certain way. As we become aware of their influence, we can choose to do things differently. The surrounding culture often prefers one side of the pole over the other, a preference that is rarely fully acknowledged. Culture surrounds us invisibly, like the air; we breathe it in unaware. As we acknowledge the influence of our history and culture, we can choose to step toward the creative midpoint, where power is born.

ORGANIZATION POLARITIES

Certain polarities particularly relevant to getting organized are explored here. Once we become aware of the influence of culture and our history we can make better choices.

Chaos/Order

Chaos and order, freedom and confinement, flexibility and rigidity, spontaneity and structure—how loaded these words are. Some structure sounds good, but rigidity doesn't. Freedom sounds great, but chaos doesn't. Defining, much less striking, a balance along this continuum is a touchy matter. We seem to operate with feet on both the brake and the accelerator when we approach issues of structure. Yes, we want it, and no, we don't.

Much of what we encounter daily is utterly unstructured. Consider what comes through the mail slot. A tax refund check for a thousand dollars lies buried under yet another invitation to change long-distance carriers. A precious letter from a long-lost friend sits beside a pet supply catalog, and we don't even have a dog! The lot is dumped on us, raw and unformed, for us to figure out. The email inbox and reams of information in magazines, newspapers, TV, or on the Web are similarly unstructured.

Yet, within this seeming chaos there is a pattern if we look deeply, simply, and clearly enough. Everything that exists has form, and all form is pattern. Without it, the stuff just wouldn't be there! The essence of getting organized is discovering that pattern and arranging our environment in such a way that the pattern shows. We tread the delicate line between being fluid and being firm.

Elsewhere/Here and Now

The "click mode" of the Internet gives the impression of instant access to everything everywhere at any time. Click on Timbuktu and we're there. Click on 16th-century Florence and we're there. It's easy to be anywhere else but here and now. Yet we, in our physical world, have to walk, ride, or drive from there to here, and covering that space takes time right now. Consciously or not, many people have bought into "click mode" and are reluctant to embrace the realities of time and space.

In an atmosphere of virtuality, we forget that every object we bring into our sphere takes up space and takes time to use, repair, store, and even get rid of. Every activity we pursue takes energy and attention. We would be wise to acknowledge these physical conditions. Rather than being frustrated, discouraged, or burdened by the conditions of life on earth, organizing can help us engage creatively with them on their own terms.

Outer/Inner

Our exterior environment of home, family, job, car, and social and civic life is where we make contact with the material world—we drive around, buy things, and meet people. We also have the capacity for an interior life where we make contact with the more-than-material world. Meditation and prayer, musing and dreaming, aspiration, artistic creation, and other spiritual practices access the unseen patterns and powers of the universe, our soul and its longings, and the Divine.

Our culture doesn't makes it easy for the interior life to flourish. Even thoughts such as goal-setting, planning, rehearsing, or reviewing are taken up with exterior concerns. To make space for the inner life, we have to beat back outer demands. A few of us have managed to create a free-standing interior life—those with an active prayer practice, meditators, fishermen, artists, runners, or gardeners. Yet even for these people, the outside world doesn't seem have a lot to do with their inner world. One is spiritual, the other mundane; one is focused, the other frantic.

Rather than waging war between the outer and the inner or keeping them separate from, and ignorant of, each other, we might have them honor, support, and inform one another. Organizing can build a bridge between them so they share a healthy, mutually informing, working relationship. As we claim our inner space and counter the pull toward the external, we allow subtle, interior information that supports getting organized to arise. We bring our outer and inner environments into harmony.

Master/Servant

American culture glorifies mastery—we are captains of our own ship; we bow to no one. According to the American dream, each person lives as s/he chooses. Indentured servitude and slavery are abolished; hereditary privilege and hierarchy are downplayed. Few of us have servants.

Difficulties arise when we fail to acknowledge that even though we don't have servants, we still need them. Being a master is not enough. We still need someone to file the papers, keep the schedule, clean the floor, and do the laundry. That someone is us. So, we need to be both good masters and good servants, and be clear when we're in each role.

The good master has an overall sense of what needs to be done and assigns work according to the capability of the servant. The master has a ready ear, praises generously, and feeds back sensitively. S/he doesn't threaten or judge. S/he is consistent. S/he protects the servant from outside pressure. The good servant is willing, able, and communicative, not balky, subversive, or unskilled. S/he doesn't deceive or malinger. The two participate in a relationship of mutual interdependence, respect, and trust. If we forget that we hold both roles when we organize, we might judge ourselves unreasonably, set poor limits, or refuse to take direction. We might not even do the work.

When master/servant roles break down—when we don't fulfill obligations or measure up to expectations—we feel shame. We think we're lazy, unmotivated, undisciplined, a slacker, or stupid. Yet often we go on as usual, without making changes or acknowledging the situation as it really is. Feeling guilty can, in some strange way, soothe us, but it doesn't always move us. We've beat ourselves up, so what more needs to be done? Nothing. However, if we act on our legitimate shame and do something to make amends, we move ahead. We build the master's capacity to direct competently and kindly, and the servant's capacity to work willingly and ably.

THE INFLUENCE OF THE SURROUNDING CULTURE

American culture today makes it difficult to get organized. In our culture, the issue of what we should do, what's right, what is the norm, is particularly fuzzy. By contrast, tight-knit tribal cultures like those of the people living in the rainforest or those of Bali or the Islamic theocracies are of whole cloth. They form a rich, continuous fabric of practices that provide an answer to every question (for good or for ill, so it appears to us). Not so in America today.

Many Rudders to Steer By
The secular idealism of the founding fathers and a gradually evolving pluralistic religious climate have given us not one but many rudders to steer by. We can see the evidence in our spiritual practices. In America today there is no one spiritual practice that contains most of what comes up for most of the people. Rather we have a dizzying array of possibilities from which to choose. We practice yoga, do Tai chi, and go to church; we consult a Reiki master, a homeopath, and an MD; we read about affirmations, out-of-body experiences, and psychology. The paths we follow are complex and rarely straight or clear. They loop back on themselves, lead into and out of dead ends, and disappear into the fog.

Our culture is porous and dilute, full of holes, gaps, and spaces for influences to creep in, inconsistencies to crop up, and questions to be raised. Cultural givens are up for grabs as we respond to situations without precedent such as for-profit health care and working mothers relying on professionals to raise their children. The culture is evolving as best it can, and, under the influence of electronics, at a breakneck pace. We are inventing ourselves at every turn—both a challenge and an opportunity.

A Mediated, Commercial Culture

Many of our cultural norms come through media—TV, talk radio, newspapers, magazines—rather than through direct interpersonal interactions played out in families and communities. The media are generally in service to profits, rather than to the ongoing evolution of humankind. Even public media like NPR or PBS are becoming permeated with a commercial presence, not to mention public schools and public transportation.

Commercial messages become cultural ones. The ads not only exhort us to buy, they also put a social, moral, and ethical spin on their messages. When they say everybody's got one, we might feel socially ostracized if we don't have one too. We might feel obligated to consume advertised products as a means of being good citizens. The ads say we deserve this product, and so we measure our sense of entitlement and self-worth by the stuff we have. We all too dutifully accept the package as offered, buying into it (as well as buying it). We say we're not prey to commercialism, but just how reliable are our filters? How much of what we believe and what we do is conditioned by commercial ends?

Commercial concerns are indeed important, as Jacob Needleman says in *Money and the Meaning of Life*. They are, nonetheless, secondary.[8] He warns that it's all too easy to make profit into a primary goal. When that happens, we're in trouble—profit's values might not support the evolution of humanity and the world. In order to participate fully in our evolution, which is what we are meant to do, we need to take up our place at the creative midpoint, which we can do only when we acknowledge commercial, cultural, and personal assumptions and counter them when necessary.

Turning Up the Heat

Much of what the commercial media asks us to do is unsustainable, if not suicidal. Consider this curious story: If you drop some frogs into a pot of boiling water, they will jump right out again. But if there's a big pot of nice, cold water, the frogs will say, "Just right." Then a very slow fire is built under the pot. In an hour the frogs say, "Mmm, this is really cozy." A while later they lay back, "Hey, this feels like Florida—great!" If the heat stays on, you end up with a pot of cooked frogs with smiles on their faces.

Change has happened so gradually that we haven't noticed how very crazy things have become. In our isolation we assume that since everybody else seems to be okay, it must just be that we're stupid or lazy or spineless. Not so!

Our snazzy electronic devices were supposed to save time and make life easier. Well, do we have more time? Is life easier? What we have instead are ever-faster turnaround times and a nonstop workweek. With a computer on every desk, we have to do it all—not just the work itself, but organizing the work too. Many of us are on our own, electronically isolated, trying to set priorities in situations where we might have five bosses, or no boss at all! No wonder we struggle with organization.

We have a wealth of information that was supposed to give us knowledge and power. It has been said that the amount of information contained in one daily issue of the *New York Times* equals the amount of print information an average literate person in the 17th century would encounter in an entire lifetime. Of course, more than three centuries have past (and what centuries of invention they were, too!). We forget, however, that the culture that ran on a *Times'* worth of information produced Shakespeare, Descartes, and Newton. Are we really that different from those folks of only a few hundred years ago? Can we really handle all this information?

BACK TO THE MIDPOINT

Many of the supports that used to make life possible to organize—a simpler life, an intact cultural fabric, interdependent relationships—just aren't there any more. Even so, we assume we can operate as if they were. The never-ending, overwhelming stream of choices, information, and just plain stuff strains our capacity to get organized. We're getting desperate; the distress signals are increasingly urgent; something *must* be done. Whenever an issue becomes so charged, it's certain that there's a lesson to be learned.

Disorganization is a sign that we've moved off the creative midpoint. We could buy into the hundreds of media programs, books, consultations, and other remedies to ease the pain and patch ourselves up. We can do what we've always done, only more, better, and faster. However, we miss an opportunity if all we do is address the immediate distress, mask symptoms, or apply Band-Aids. More-better-faster isn't the answer. A deep change in our approach to the whole question is.

Getting organized is as much a call to pay attention to our souls as it is to attend to our stuff. We need to find new ways of doing things—ones that stay in contact with our true selves in the midst of our complicated lives. Practices such as those explored here establish a connection between the everyday details of our lives and the soul movements that work below the surface, behind the scenes, beyond and through the details. These practices get us back to the creative midpoint.

Making Our Own Way

Because of the gaps in our culture, its willingness to borrow, and the speed with which it changes, we have an opportunity to make our own way. We can go with the culture or not, assume what the culture assumes or not, expect what the culture expects or not. We can, and indeed must, if we are to live sustainably, question what the culture offers at every turn.

When we accept the package as offered, we might earnestly believe that we're making the "right" choice; after all, that's what's expected. However, a diet of only one kind of food, even so-called good food, is not only dull but also unhealthy. Similarly, acquaintances who think like we do not only bore us but also isolate us. A life that operates on only one side of the polarity, be it culturally sanctioned or not, might not be good for us.

Say we strive for improvement. Improvement is good, right? However, continually improving neglects the need to integrate our gains. Pain is bad, right? Yet if we mask pain with drugs, we might ignore the vital signals it sends. Productivity is good, right? However, fallow times are worthy too. This is not to say that all values are relative. Most of us have a moral code that tells us, without question, that some things are right and others are wrong.

Our choices can be determined less by the received cultural (and/or commercial) package than by the prompting of our souls. We learn that desire itself is not the problem, but rather, desires that have no end—the cravings that the product promoters bank will never and can never be satisfied. True desire, on the other hand, orients us rightly to exactly what we need, which, when we get it, will satisfy.

We come to see that our culture's norms are but one set of many, particular to this time and place; and that they will shift, change, and eventually pass away. The laws of the universe, on the other hand, endure, regardless of the cultural package. We can choose to orient our life by universal law and the soul's desire, serving a pattern much larger than our particular culture. We become free agents, fully responsible for the situations we find ourselves in, without excuses, paralyzing guilt, or elaborate justification.

As we venture out beyond the safety of the received culture, like the Inuit in the tundra beyond the range of his clan, we are wisely alert, calling on knowledge, skills, courage, and most of all, trust. We trust that universal law and the soul's desire will make themselves known to us, if we but listen. We trust that paying attention to them will orient us rightly. Then we find security within ourselves, knowing deep in our bones that we are part of the grand pattern, whether we buy into the package or not.

Restoring Balance

If we want to make good choices about how we organize ourselves, we need to get back to the balance point at the middle of the polarity poles. When we think of balance, we often envision a peaceful, quiet state. But balance is anything but quiet. The tightrope walker, apparently calm, is in fact continually adjusting, compensating, and responding to influences, both inner and outer, to maintain a delicate and ever-fleeting balance. Dynamism of the highest order happens at that place between the poles.

To rekindle vitality, we need first to become aware that something is off. Dullness, heaviness, and lack of zest are all signs. If we hear ourselves say, "I'm too busy to get organized; I have more important things to do," or, "If I pay attention to myself, I'll let my family (or coworkers) down," more than likely, it's a sign that we're no longer at the midpoint.

Thomas Moore, in his book *The Re-Enchantment of Everyday Life*, points out that "we don't think we have control over the engine of our own hyperactivity. . . We seem to be victims of evolutionary processes instead of makers and artists of our own culture and individual lives."[9] We've bought the package and feel trapped within it. Moore calls us to counter destructive cultural tendencies "positively by turning our backs to the disenchanted values that dominate modern life"[10]—busyness, productivity, and the accumulation of stuff.

We restore balance by refusing to let the flashy, disenchanted side captivate us and by fostering intensity and vividness in the weaker, less culturally supported side. We remember that in a dynamic dance, overdeveloped muscles are as much a hindrance as underdeveloped ones, so we back off from the strong side while we build up the weak.

At times, operating according to one side of the pole is appropriate, at other times, the other. Sometimes it is wise to charge forth; other times, to hold back. Wisdom literature advises, "to every thing there is a season."[11] Our job is, first, to be open to a choice; next, to discern what is called for when; and then, to make our choice and act. Then we dance like the tightrope ballerina.

Skills for Handling Options
Opening Them Up and Settling Them Down

OUR PHYSICAL WORLD imposes absolute constraints of time and space. We have only so much time in which to do everything we're supposed to do, expected to do, or want to do. We have only so much space in which to fit our stuff—our bookshelves, wall space, and closets are so large and no larger. On the other hand, our thoughts and desires are endless. We can imagine what it would be like to fly in a spacecraft to the other side of the moon. We can entertain all kinds of possibilities for a free Saturday afternoon.

LIMITED/LIMITLESS

Our lives happen between the limited world and our limitless thoughts and aspirations. We might desire to travel, yet at the same time, we want to stay close to home and build community. We want to both play and work on Saturday, yet the few hours of time and our reserve of energy constrains what we might do.

The skills in this group, Imagining and Choosing, help us navigate between both sides of the issue of limits. In Imagining we loosen our attachment to limitation so the imagination can run free. We receive from the font of all possibilities. In Choosing we learn how to bear the fact that our choices, which we necessarily make all the time, have consequences. We learn how to put aside the options that we must reject with consciousness and grace.

Conscious attention to both sides of the options issue brings us face to face with our essential human condition—as *both/and*, rather than *either/or* beings. If even for a moment we entertain simultaneous awareness of both our limits and our limitlessness, we make that bridge between our two natures, the spiritual and the mundane. Option Skills allow us to explore both the limited earth and the limitless sky. In so doing, we experience the powerful paradox at the root of our being.

OPTION SKILL CATCHPHRASES

Eagle View/Ant View
Foreground/Background
Opportunity Cost
(See page 181 for definitions.)

Everyday Imagining

We use Imagining when we

    leaf through magazines cruising for ideas

    picture ourselves in relationship with someone we don't know or in a job we don't have

    do speculative travel planning

    put on a costume and act as another person

Spiritual Imagining

We use Imagining when we

    let ourselves be open to signs, synchronicities, serendipity

    feel ourselves part of a much larger pattern

    note our attractions

    explore a "past life"

    take on the persona of an animal, plant, or stone

II. Imagining
Opening Up Options

OUR PHYSICAL WORLD imposes absolute constraints. Yet, at the same time, we have the capacity to venture far beyond these constraints through boundless imagination and endless creativity. We can make contact with the infinite spirit that interpenetrates the limited world we see and touch. Our ability to go beyond earthly limits may in fact help us work within the limits of time and space in new ways.

ABUNDANCE

The other side of Nature's constraints of time and space is its bounteous fecundity. There are millions of spores in a single puff from a mushroom, thousands of eggs in the salmon's belly, countless variations on clouds in the sky. Nature offers seemingly endless permutations on what might happen—this fish or that, this color of flower or that.

Mirroring Nature's abundance, we practice Imagining, generating countless alternatives, loosening our vise-grip on a particular way of doing things. We don't have to do it this one way, or my way, or even the right way. Through Imagining we see there are many ways, each with value. We bring an element of fantasy and play into our work. We feel the hope, delight, and awe that come from making contact with the limitless. We move forward, in touch with the creative flow of experience in our lives.

Stumped and Stopped
Sometimes we know exactly what to do. We're moving along in the river of experience. Other times we don't. It may be a question of ignorance—say we have no experience setting up a home office or we never had to deal with bills before. It may be a question of confusion—we fumble around in a resistance-induced fog, desperately grasping for answers.

When we're stumped and stopped, Imagining can shake things up so we can get moving again. We step out of the dammed-up river of experience, do a little Imagining, and then step back in. We get a fresh perspective and access knowledge that was there all along although not easily available.

IMAGINING IN ACTION

Imagining opens us to new perceptions and ways of being by loosening our connections to the obvious, workaday, and predictable. There are countless ways to practice Imagining. Looking in the library catalogue or searching the Internet under "creativity" or "creative problem solving" leads to plenty of resources, some of which are in the the resource section on *page 191*. We will explore three techniques here: brainstorming—used in many conventional contexts to awaken the imagination; daydreaming—which brings fantasy and visualization into play; and bricolage (French for "hardware" or "jerry-rigging")—which makes use of whatever comes to hand for the answer to our question.

Brainstorming

Classic brainstorming is a three-stage process whose steps are:

1. Set the intention/Loosen attachments
2. Generate and capture ideas
3. Reflect on the options/Choose a course of action

Set the Intention/Loosen Attachments

When we set an intention for our brainstorm, we give our imagining self an arena in which to play. The brainstorming process can take us very far afield—indeed, that's exactly what we want. Yet, we also want a place to return to. We formulate a simple sentence that states our intention simply and clearly. For example, if we want to make bill paying easier, we might say, "My intention for this session is to come up with ideas for paying the bills." We need not keep the intention in mind while we brainstorm. Our imagining self does that for us. We can be as free-wheeling as possible and trust that whatever comes will be useful in some way.

We loosen attachments to conventional solutions by entertaining whatever ideas come to mind. Every idea is welcome at the brainstorm party, no matter how off-the-wall, outrageous, or impractical. There is no sentry at the door checking the guest list.

We loosen our attachment to history. We set aside how it's been done in the past, because, after all, we're looking for something entirely new. We loosen our attachment to personal experience, refusing to let past failures short-circuit the free flow of ideas. We loosen our attachments to social norms. It doesn't matter how our ideas look to others or even to ourselves. We loosen our attachment to limits of time, money, and space. Anything goes!

Generate and Capture Ideas

We heat up our brainstorming session by putting it in a strong container and building the fire of imagination under it. The container is a time limit. The best ideas often come in the very last minutes of the time allotted. If there's no time limit, there are no "last minutes." Putting a back boundary on the session makes that "last-ditch effort" possible.

The session heats up considerably when we enlist others to join in. Even one other "imaginer" in the room with whom to bounce ideas around generates electric sparks and flashes of insight. The "no-judgment, anything-goes" rule heats up the brainstorm as well. Leave the cold censor at the door.

We set up in advance a means to capture the creative ideas as they arise. The best method is to have someone who's not participating in the brainstorm post ideas on large sheets of paper. The material is instantly available to everyone so ideas can build on one another and spark new options. In solo brainstorming we might write furiously on a large sheet of paper for the set amount of time. Alternatively, we can video- or audio-tape the session. If we don't have to remember the ideas as well as generate them, we can give ourselves more fully to the brainstorm. With the ideas written down or taped, we can more easily do the next steps of reflecting on and choosing an idea.

Reflect on the Options/Choose a Course of Action.

Sometimes during a brainstorm, the Perfect Solution appears. There's no question about which action to take—problem solved! More often, however, after the intense heat of the brainstorm, we sort through the ideas we've generated. The Shedding and Sorting processes identify possible solutions.

See Shedding, page 111 and Sorting, page 75

We would be wise not to dismiss outrageous ideas out of hand. They often have a bit of gold in them. Say, in a brainstorm about cleaning out the garage, one idea was "Call in the National Guard." Certainly in the form it came to us, it's an impossible idea. However, if we let the idea swirl around a while, some components might be perfectly workable. We might "conscript" our teenage son and his friends (with suitable incentives) as our garage-cleaning infantrymen. We might hire the basketball coach as supervising sergeant. We might have a "situation room" meeting with some of the friends' parents to devise a strategy. Calling in the National Guard is, in some sense, a perfect solution.

As we reflect on the options after a free-wheeling brainstorm session, we see how our habits and assumptions have limited our imagination, how every idea would have had to pass through a number of filters before it came to light. Loosening our attachments shows what our assumptions have been.

See Choosing, page 143

Once we recognize the assumptions, we can choose to set them aside. We might have assumed that storage goes in boxes, but now we can consider hanging bags of seasonal decorations from the ceiling of the closet. We might have always done everything ourselves, but now we can consider getting help from our family or community. We might have assumed that no one in our circle would hire a servant, but now we can consider hiring someone to run errands for us. Setting assumptions aside opens up possibilities.

See Shedding, page 111 and Choosing, page 143

See Beginning, page 53 and Ending, page 41

Once we've identified some possibilities, other organizing skills can kick in. When there are several viable options, we can use the Shedding and the Choosing Skills to narrow them down. Once we've made the choice, we can use Threshold Skills to identify a good place to start and make a strong time container for our work. We can break the project down into manageable tasks and proceed from there.

Daydreaming

Daydreaming is another imagining technique that accesses ideas floating just underneath our consciousness. It uses elements of brainstorming and creative visualization. As in brainstorming, we define our question. Then, we visualize a mental image of it. In our mind's eye, we actively build a detailed vision of the area to address, not in words but in images, most often with eyes closed, sitting or lying in a comfortable position.

For example, our question might be how to proceed with organizing our desk. We visualize the papers on the desk in detail, where they're placed, the size and shape of the stacks, the other objects. We sense the quality of light in the room, the feel of the air, the ambient sounds.

Then, rather than generating options as in brainstorming, we open ourselves to receive a message on how to proceed. We are receptive rather than active. As in Observing, we practice open attention—we don't figure out, plan, or analyze. We merely open our daydreaming self to receive whatever message may come.

The solution to the question may come as a clear directive or it may be veiled in symbol *(see Resources: dream dictionary, page 192).* It may be a feeling or movement rather than a picture or word. In the case of organizing the desk, we may hear a reveille bugle call—first thing in the morning might be the message. Or perhaps a particular pile of papers will stand out in color with the rest of the picture in black and white—here's the place to start. Or we may see a line of ants each carrying one grain of wheat—do a little bit at a time. We can trust that whatever meaning we intuit the message to hold is sufficient. If several options arise, we can make an active choice or leave the decision to a divination tool *(see Resources: Divination, page 192).*

Bricolage

Bricolage is a third imagining technique that creates what we need from whatever materials come to hand. Some might call it jerry-rigging. Others call it making do. Oftentimes in organizing, we get into thinking, "Oh, if I only had a three-drawer file cabinet, everything would be fine," or, "I really need a fancy planner in order to manage my time." Well, that may be so. The cabinet or the planner may be the perfectly appropriate tool that will indeed make organizing very much easier. However, we would be wise to be wary. "If only" thinking—looking for the solutions elsewhere—may be an anxious cover for resistance. If that's so, no file cabinet or special planner will help. When it's a question of resistance, the best we can do might be to take whatever comes to hand and just use it.

The shoe box may indeed be a perfectly adequate staging tool for the bills. We needn't trot out to the specialty store for a wire-mesh bill holder. We can attach an unused basket to the back door for staging the outgoing mail. The old trunk may be the right size for storing children's art projects, as well as having the appropriate character of a repository of memories.

Bricolage allows us to see things afresh. The familiar things we're so used to seeing take on a new personality. It's like going to a party with an old friend and in the new setting, seeing a side of him or her we'd never encountered before. Bricolage loosens up rigid expectations and habitual perceptions.

GIFTS OF IMAGINING

Imagining helps us step back from our situation. We bracket our immediate concerns and take an excursion into another realm where we look back at the situation from a whole new angle. We see our problem as a fascinating puzzle, a challenging game, an opportunity to exercise creativity, ingenuity, and intuition. Imagining helps us access interest, and even delight.

See
Observing,
page 21

Besides being fun, the very act of Imagining puts us in the same slightly detached, yet interested position that we assume when Observing. We have access not only to the distressing situation before us but also to infinite resources beyond the distress.

Imagining promotes flexibility and responsiveness. We see not just one solution to our problem but many. We find we have a much greater range than we thought. We touch all levels of experience, diving down into the matrix of all possibilities, swirling around in boundless knowledge, flying with the angels. We are bigger than our problem.

Brainstorming

The three steps of brainstorming are:

1. Set the intention/Loosen attachments

2. Generate and capture ideas

3. Reflect on the options/Choose a course of action

This practice sheet leads you through the steps.

Set the Intention/Loosen Attachments

Stating what you want out of the session gives the imagining self an arena in which to work. The intention is a sentence, such as, "My intention for this brainstorm session is to identify ways to store my craft supplies appropriately." Be aware of the level of detail in your intention. If it's too broad (say, to identify appropriate places for everything in the house), you may need to narrow it down. If it's too narrow (say, to find the perfect place for brushes in the bookcase), you may block out creative responses that aren't within your intention. Loosen your attachment to history, preconceptions, and expectations to let the brainstorming ideas flow freely.

My intention for this brainstorm session is:

_____

_____

_____

_____

Generate and Capture Ideas

In brainstorming you set aside preconceived notions, make a container for the session, generate heat, and capture whatever comes up.

✦ Any idea is welcome—silly, smart, nonsensical, impractical, embarrassing. In such an atmosphere ideas can flow freely.

✦ Give the session a time limit. Ten minutes is a good lower limit. With less than that you hardly have an opportunity to get past the obvious. A half hour is an upper limit. With more than that you lose focus. Fifteen to twenty minutes is best for most brainstorms.

✦ Enlisting others is the best way to generate heat. Make sure the "no-judgment" rule is clear to everyone. Ideas often build one on another. Be ready for that.

✦ Before beginning have a mechanism in place to capture the ideas. Video- or audio-tape the session; post ideas on large sheets of paper on the walls; scribble as you go, making sure that you don't let the writing process cool off the brainstorm.

Reflect on the Options/Choose a Course of Action

When the time limit is up, step back to identify useful material. "Gold" can be embedded in fanciful, impractical ideas; let your imagining self help you find it.

Highlight good ideas with color, connect similar thoughts, and give shape to the ideas. The *80/20 Rule* says that 80 percent of the significance resides in only 20 percent of the possibilities, so bring the most workable options into the foreground and let the rest recede into the background.

Once you've chosen a course of action, bring in the Threshold Skills to get you started.

Daydreaming

In daydreaming you make use of the half-awake/half-asleep state where fantasy runs free. This is the place where wonderful solutions are bestowed upon you from "who-knows-where." The steps of daydreaming are similar to those of brainstorming. They are:

1. Formulate the intention and prepare

2. Go into daydreaming and capture the ideas and images

3. Reflect on the options and choose a course of action

1. Formulate the Intention, Prepare, Set a Time Limit

✦ Intention: State your intention for the vision in a simple sentence, such as, "My intention for this daydreaming session is to come up with ways to deal with the photographs."

✦ Prepare: Before you start, it's wise to prepare yourself for whatever comes up. Daydreams can be strange, mysterious, even disturbing, just like night dreams. Any intense images that come up are more to grab your attention than to scare you. Realize that all messages serve your intention. Despite their oddity, they have something valuable to offer.

✦ Timer: Use an external time-limiting mechanism so you don't have to keep track of time while you daydream. You may time the session by playing a piece of music or set a gentle alarm. Daydreaming at twilight can be particularly pleasant. As darkness deepens, images float up. You may lie down or sit comfortably in a chair. You may do a conscious relaxation process to let go of muscle tension and intruding thoughts.

2. Go into Daydreaming and Capture the Ideas and Images

✦ daydream: Allow yourself to drift into daydreaming for the allotted time.

✦ Capture ideas: Use the detached Observing Skill to note whatever comes. Capture the ideas and images on tape or with pen and paper. You might have a clipboard with blank sheets of paper handy. If you're lying down in the dark, place the clipboard on your stomach or chest and, without getting up, write a word or two to trigger your memory. Use the thumb of your other hand as a guide so you won't write over what you've already written. Begin one line next to your thumb, then move your thumb down for the next line and write next to that.

3. Reflect on the Options and Choose a Course of Action

✦ Move out of daydreaming at the end of the allotted time and gently move into reflection mode. In daydreaming for a solution to a question, it helps to have a light hand. Dream images can sometimes have an intense, fateful aspect to them. Remember, the exercise is in service to a particular situation. Glean what you can to address the situation and leave the rest. A dream dictionary may help you decipher symbols and curious images *(see Resources: dream dictionary, page 192)*.

✦ You can use your good sense, your intuition, the Decision Sieve practice sheet in the Choosing chapter *(see page 143)*, or a divination method *(see Resources: Divination, page 192)* to identify an option to go with. Then use the Threshold Skills to begin the work.

You can use the same procedure for night dreaming as well. Formulate the intention before retiring and capture the images on arising.

Bricolage

Bricolage is puttering around and taking whatever comes to hand to solve a problem. Bricolage may generate perfectly adequate, even elegant solutions. More than that, it frees our imagination and loosens our hold on packaged notions of what's supposed to work. Use this practice sheet to write out an experience of bricolage.

Identify the Problem
What are you trying to do?

_____

_____

_____

Putter Around and Take What Comes to Hand
Park the problem in the back of your mind and putter around for a time—maybe an hour, maybe a week. Keep your feelers out for anything that might possibly work. Whatever attracts your attention or comes to hand is worthy material. Consider everything. Try it all out. Modify it if necessary. You can use this space to list your bricolage possibilities.

_____

_____

_____

Gather Feedback
What was the kernel of the solution to the problem? If what you've come up with from bricolage doesn't serve, what would?

_____

_____

_____

Everyday Choosing

We use Choosing when we

    look through a menu and decide what not to have, as well as what to have

    get dressed for the day, choosing among many possible outfits

    decide to go with a particular theme in interior decorating, which eliminates some options

    choose among several equally interesting possibilities for Saturday night entertainment

    alter plans in response to the weather

Spiritual Choosing

We use Choosing when we

    acknowledge the consequences of not following our conscience

    follow our inner guide, even though it might be uncomfortable

    embrace wholeness—bright and dark sides—rather than only part of ourselves

    settle down feelings of shame and guilt concerning life path decisions

I2. Choosing
Settling Down Options

WE MAKE CHOICES all the time, every moment of every day. We choose to get up rather than sleep in. We eat oatmeal for breakfast rather than corn flakes. We wear the blue shirt rather than the white one. And so on. We are constantly choosing, influenced by a wide range of factors—our past experience, our desires, the media, our immediate family or associates, our intuition, our ethics, the requirements of the task.

CHOICES—BOTH EASY AND DIFFICULT

Even though we choose all the time, we're only occasionally aware that we are doing it. Most choices seem automatic; they're clear, simple, and easy. We know what we want. We've done it this way before. We're clear on the right course of action. All the signs point in the same direction.

Other choices are complex, fateful, and fraught with difficulty. They're not so clear, obvious, and pure. Do we even know what we want? We might have no experience with the kind of thing we're choosing, or too much of the wrong kind of experience. In a lesser-of-two-evils choice, can we know what's best? In a choice between equally good options, can we let go of the rejected option? We're tentative; we vacillate. Even if we do make a choice, we backslide or have second thoughts.

Ambivalence Brings Awareness

Difficult choices call forth awareness. Ultimately, as active, forward-facing beings, we are going to move, somehow, somewhere. The challenge is to use the opportunity a difficult choice presents and choose with awareness.

Too Many Choices

The media and our consumer culture give us ready access to a wealth of possibilities. For example, magazines tell us about the different kinds of exercise we might take up. Catalogs offer us hundreds of styles of chairs. The Internet gives us information about what house plants we might buy. Does access to all this information make it easier to choose? Probably not. Instead we get stuck at the choice point, pulled in several directions at once, unable to decide which way to go.

With so many confusing options to sort out, we'd just as soon let someone else decide. The purveyors of the options, of course, are all too eager to have us put our choices in their hands. Those around us in our family, job, and community also have their agendas for our choices. In the absence of compelling evidence from within ourselves, at least having them decide gets us off the mark. The trouble comes when, having accepted their choice on one level, we still balk at it. We don't go with it wholeheartedly. We're still, in some way, on the fence.

When we habitually base our choices on the expectations of others—be they family, work associates, the media, or commercial purveyors—we don't give our own capacity to choose the chance to develop. Since we will not read everything, do everything, or get everything we or anyone else would want us to, we would be wise to learn how to choose skillfully. We raise the issue for ourselves, explore the challenge in the choice, and resolve it enough to move forward.

Involve the Entire Self

The rational way to choose is to thoroughly investigate all the possibilities, gather all the information, and make a reasoned decision. Sounds good, but is it really wise to base choices solely on rationality? We have other "selves" besides our thinking self, and they would like a say in the matter. In fact, if they don't get a say, they may sabotage the choice. The thinking self, always the strong one in our culture, may muscle its choice through saying, "I've made my decision and that's that." The excluded emotional self may then have regrets and second thoughts. The intuitive self senses trouble and keeps us from acting on the decision. These are signs that not all of our selves have been consulted.

The two-part choosing process described below explores the feeling self's involvement in making choices. As for the intuiting self, paying attention to hunches, dreams, and fantasies allows for its input. We can also involve "selves" beyond our personality through prayer, meditation, and divination *(see Resources: Divination, page 192).*

Identifying a Choice Is Not Enough

The Choosing Skill is not so much about identifying which option to choose, but rather discovering the implications of following through on the choice. Techniques like the Yes/No/Maybe Shedding exercise *(see page 117)*, or even flipping a coin can provide a viable option. That's not the difficult part. The problem is that once we've made the choice, we fixate on the option we're trying to bring into our life. We think about it, dream about it, visualize it, and affirm it—which doesn't sound problematic. However, there's another side to the issue which, if we ignore it, will get us into trouble.

Consider this situation with exercise. We might resolve to go to the gym twice a week. "Yes! I will go to the gym. Yes! Yes! Yes!" we repeat daily. We think positively. We affirm our intention to exercise. But somehow we don't show up at the gym. In order to actually move ahead we need to be able to say, "No, I'm not going to be able to catch up on my paperwork here at the office," "No, I'm not going to meet my friend for tea," "No, I'm not going to remain cool and dry."

In order to say Yes, we have to say No to all the other options. And saying No certainly isn't easy. The issue is encapsulated in a principle from economics called the *Opportunity Cost,* which says, "The true cost of something is what we have to give up in order to get it." If we neglect paying proper attention to what we are giving up, we risk sabotaging the whole effort. Instead, we make peace with our old ways in order to move on to new ones. We get an appreciation of what it costs to get what we want, and then decide if we're willing to pay.

CHOOSING IN ACTION

In Choosing we generate a list of what we would have to leave behind and then make peace with each item. This process clears the way for the choice to take hold. It settles down our ambivalence, clarifies what is really important to us, and prepares us to bear the consequences of our choices.

Imagine the Change Has Already Happened

In order to call forth what we would be giving up should we change, first we build in our imagination a sense that the change has already occurred. We imagine that the problem is solved. Then we pay attention to the thoughts, feelings, and images that arise when in this new state. We note all the things that would be difficult to give up.

Using getting organized as an example, we imagine that we're organized—completely and totally. Everything is exactly as we would like it to be. Although this sounds like heaven, such a change brings up plenty of issues that are not so easy to leave behind. Here are some of them:

+ We might leave behind an image of ourselves that we've entertained for a long·time; just who are we if not disorganized?
+ Others may also have an image of us we'd be abandoning ("Oh, she's the disorganized one in the family"). How does that influence interpersonal dynamics?
+ We would leave behind a familiar, although perhaps not comfortable, way of operating. Learning new behaviors is awkward, and even embarrassing.
+ Being disorganized is an all-purpose excuse behind which to hide. When we're disorganized we don't have to be so accountable. When we're disorganized, people don't pile on more work. Should we be organized, we'll have no excuses and be open to an onslaught of work.
+ If we were organized, we would know what our best efforts actually are; we could no longer say, "I would've done better, but I was swamped."
+ Should we become organized, we would see our priorities reflected back to us. For instance, it would be obvious that hiking is no longer as important as it once was; can we let that go? Or, we might choose clothes that are comfortable now over those we hope to fit into someday; can we live with our actual, rather than ideal, body?
+ Not only would we see our priorities, everybody else would see them too. We might find that a particular relationship doesn't serve our greater good and decide to pull back from it; can we stand what our friend may feel in the face of that?

We flesh out the list as fully as possible. Brainstorming with a sympathetic friend can stimulate other ideas and help us stay with the process. If we do it alone, we can tape the session or write on blank sheets of paper to capture the items.

See
Imagining,
page 131

Often the most telling items are found underneath the more obvious ones. For example, we feel that being organized would make us give up spontaneity, freedom, and creativity—certainly difficult to give up. If we probe further we see that underneath that is a fear of being rigid like Aunt Martha; underneath that is a fear of boredom, and underneath that is anxiety about exactly what we are to do in this world.

Make Peace with What We Leave Behind

Choosing exposes the underside of our choice. The bright, shiny, Yes side—the change we seek—is only part of the picture. When we turn over the bright side of the rock, we see what goes along with it—the dark, complex side that rarely sees the light of day. Choosing brings us face to face with shadow parts of ourselves that move and drive us, most often unconsciously.

These hidden aspects have value. We're wise not to harshly suppress, negate, or toss them away. The spontaneity, freedom, and creativity we fear to leave behind should we get organized are good things. So is having excuses at the ready when we're called upon to do something we'd rather not. Most of what we find under the rock is, or has been, adaptive in some way. There's a reason for our reluctance to change

Fear of What Might Happen, Not What Will Happen

As we uncover what we might give up in order to change, we begin to sense that it's not what *would actually* happen that's the problem, so much as what we fear *might* happen. The horrors we identify wouldn't have to occur. None of them, in fact, need happen.

For example, in the getting organized case, if we've identified that spontaneity would be hard to give up, there's nothing that says that we can't be both spontaneous and organized. Knowing how important spontaneity is to us, we can be sure to foster it in our life even as we get more organized. Say we use disorganization to insulate ourselves from more work. We can develop communication skills and a sense of realistic demands so that we don't have to hide behind our chaos.

The dark issues can sabotage our good efforts if we ignore them. If we respect them, we find that each carries a nugget of truth. If we acknowledge that truth, we don't have to hold back. We listen to what each issue has to offer, incorporate its lessons into our new way of being, and then move on.

Laying Down New Tracks

Choosing a different way of operating softens up old habits. When we choose not to do things as we've always done, we step out of the deep groove in our behavior that our habits have laid down. New possibilities open up. The territory, though unfamiliar, and perhaps frightening, is nonetheless fresh and unmarked. We have the opportunity to see things in a new way.

For example, our habitual way of organizing might be to get all fired up and do it in a blaze of white-hot activity. Of course, this method does work—it confines organizing to a single session and offers great satisfaction at the end. That's why we continue to do it. However, we don't maintain the steady level of organization that we'd like, and we need special conditions—a long stretch of time in which to work, and considerable physical, mental, and emotional energy that needs to be replenished when we're done. Nonetheless, we've laid down a groove in our behavior that's difficult to step out of.

Bless the Old Way, and Move On

The behaviors that have served us in the past aren't stupid or silly. They've given us real gifts that we would be wise to honor. The positive benefit of our new way of operating doesn't negate the virtue of the old way. It's not a matter of toting up the negatives and positives against one another. We embrace our past and honor it. In so doing we act kindly with ourselves and our process.

These old grooves in our behavior furnish a valuable counterweight to forward progress. They insist that we fully integrate the new way on a deeper level and not just the surface. They prod us to uncover the hidden side of our choices so that we don't miss the full range of lessons the choices present to us. We can rely on our troublesome behaviors—our habits, compulsions, and addictions—to provide a steady source of material to work on and bless them as our greatest teachers.

Still, we choose to move on. That was then; this is now. No doubt, ten years from now, we will look back at the new ways of operating we're putting in place right here and say the same: that was then; this is now. In order to do things differently from this point forward, we make peace with our old ways, and then leave them.

Choosing and Will

With choices before us every moment of our lives, we can ask, "What, in this moment, shall I do, think, say, or feel? Is this my choice? Is this my will?" We choose where to lend our attention. We choose our thoughts, words, and actions. We choose, perhaps, not so much our feelings, but certainly our response to our feelings.

As we continue, we come to know our will. We find what we really want. As we build our capacity, we can decide to make our choices in harmony with our deep alignments. We may well sacrifice our own will for the sake of our fellows, or the planet, or the Highest Good. As we become free, then we can willingly become bound.

What Do I Give Up?

This two-part choosing process first identifies what you would have to give up should you make a change, and then makes peace with what you would be leaving behind. It clears the way for the choice to take hold by settling down ambivalence and, in the process, clarifying what is important.

Imagine the Change Has Already Happened and Let the Difficulties Arise
Build up in your imagination a sense that the change has already occurred. The change is in place; the problem is solved. Imagine yourself in the new situation, doing the new behavior.

Next, pay attention to whatever thoughts, feelings, and images arise in this new state that would be difficult to give up were the problem solved. Uncover as many difficulties as possible and list them below. For example, you might imagine your files perfectly organized. If that were so, you'd have no excuse if you couldn't find something; you'd have to be accountable.

_____   _____

_____   _____

_____   _____

_____   _____

_____   _____

Make Peace with What We Leave Behind
Now, look back over the list and settle down each item.
+ Ask—Can I stand it? Can I bear the fact that I'm not perfect or that others are going to have to help out or that I won't have the confusion of disorganization to hide behind?
+ Ask—Would I actually have to leave this behind or can I get some of what I would miss?

In the example above, you might accept that even with a "perfect" system, you can cut yourself some slack and not have to be "perfectly" accountable. Much of what we fear to leave behind is, or has been, valuable in some way. Identify the value in the difficulties and creatively build it into your solution.

Decision Sieve

Here is a no-brainer way to reveal your preferences when faced with a decision. Just go through the steps mindlessly and see what happens. If all else fails, flip a coin.

Step 1.
Assign each option a number. Then compare each option, one at a time, to every other one, using the grid below. Circle the option you prefer in each pair.

1	1	1	1	1	1	1	1
2	3	4	5	6	7	8	9
	2	2	2	2	2	2	2
	3	4	5	6	7	8	9
		3	3	3	3	3	3
		4	5	6	7	8	9
			4	4	4	4	4
			5	6	7	8	9
				5	5	5	5
				6	7	8	9
					6	6	6
					7	8	9
						7	7
						8	9
							8
							9

Step 2.

Count how many times you circled each option; enter that number for each below:

1: _____   2: _____   3: _____   4: _____   5: _____   6: _____   7: _____   8: _____   9: _____

Step 3.

Arrange the options in order of the most votes:

1st choice: _____   **4th choice:** _____   **7th choice:** _____

2nd choice: _____   **5th choice:** _____   **8th choice:** _____

3rd choice: _____   **6th choice:** _____   **9th choice:** _____

Skills to Carry On
Placing Organizing in Context

THE SKILLS OF THIS SECTION, Sustaining and Engaging, place organizing in context. By these skills we carry all the other skills into our daily lives. Sustaining brings organizing to the foreground by regularly attending to the maintenance tasks that keep our systems energized, vital, and operating smoothly. Engaging lets organizing operate continuously in the background, where it supports and upholds us, mediating between the world before us and the world within and beyond us.

EVER-EXPANDING RELATIONSHIP

Working with our stuff, we work at relationship. We become skillful at relating all of our stuff to all of our thoughts, feelings, and actions. We welcome everything, including troublesome thoughts, uncomfortable feelings, and difficult situations. We address the challenges with skill, knowing that within those challenges our most valuable lessons lie. Rather than trying to get rid of them, we embrace them, and, in so doing, enfold our total experience into our organizing systems. We develop accountability and responsibility, as well as tenderness and compassion toward our stuff and ourselves.

Aligning with Nature

Through organizing we come into alignment with how Nature works and so are carried forth on its current. Life becomes less of a struggle and more of a river-raft ride, which the skills help us navigate with grace. The harmonious relationship between our stuff and our way of being opens a channel through which messages from the more than-human world can enter. We are open to the influence of the universe, which lends us power to engage fully and effectively.

CARRYING-ON SKILLS CATCHPHRASES

Follow the Deeper Rhythm
From This Moment On
Holographic Organization
Start Small
2 Steps Forward/1 Step Back
(See page 181 for definitions.)

Everyday Sustaining

We use Sustaining when we

    brush our teeth every day

    do the laundry

    repair the car when it breaks down

    get dressed in the morning and undressed at night

Spiritual Sustaining

We use Sustaining when we

    maintain relationships through visits, calls, and letters

    do any hobby or activity as a regular spiritual practice, even when we don't "want" to

    notice when we're "off" and take a walk, go to a museum, or practice a sport to right ourselves

    refresh and renew contact with our purpose in life

I3 • Sustaining
Renewing the System

THE HALLMARK of a living system is that it continually renews itself. Every cell in our body participates in the process of dying and being reborn, breaking down and building up. As skin is sloughed off, new skin is uncovered below. We take in food, break it down, separate out what our body needs, and throw off the rest. The vigor of the system depends on how well it renews itself. If the renewal process is compromised, well-being is compromised.

A NATURAL PROCESS

Organizing mirrors natural processes—the rhythmic ebb and flow of spreading out and gathering in, acquiring and letting go. We refresh our pile of decisions by handling and considering each piece, sloughing off some, keeping others. We take in the mail and funnel it through our staging tools, sending it on its proper path. We periodically review the efficacy of our systems and adjust them accordingly. Our systems depend on renewal for their continued well-being.

The Negative Spin on Maintenance
Renewing and refreshing sounds wonderful. The fact remains, however, that what we're talking about is maintenance work—in a class with cleaning toilets and collecting garbage. These are not activities most of us relish or seek out. Still, they're absolutely necessary.

There was a time when "others" (whoever was so deemed in the culture) did maintenance work—servants, women, and other helpers. Now, we assume both roles: the Master—the producer of ideas, goods, and actions—and the Servant—the maintainer of the systems that support the ideas, goods, and actions. The interlude on organization polarities *(see page 119)* lays out the two roles and how they interact within us.

Maintenance might seem distasteful, demeaning, and shameful. We counter this negative atmosphere by seeing it as the refreshing function it actually is. When we pay proper attention to maintenance using the Sustaining Skills in this chapter, we make the tasks easier to do, more comfortable, even pleasant. Then we can do maintenance honorably, appropriately, and with good cheer.

SUSTAINING IN ACTION

Three areas to consider when Sustaining are: identifying the appropriate tasks to do, doing them with appropriate timing and intensity, and using appropriate tools.

What to Do

Each organizing system asks for renewal in its own way. Looking at our stuff, we ask, what keeps stuff flowing through the system? Although the specifics are different for each person, many of us do similar maintenance tasks. Here are some examples:

- ✦ sort incoming mail
- ✦ do maintenance reading—memos, correspondence, email, journals
- ✦ respond to communications
- ✦ decide what to do, buy, or read
- ✦ file
- ✦ schedule and plan
- ✦ throw stuff away
- ✦ revisit "things to do later"

Observing,
page 21

The practice sheets list these and other possible maintenance tasks. Not everyone does all the tasks. We call on our observer to help us identify what we need to do to maintain our unique way of operating on a regular basis.

When to Do It—Timing and Intensity

The timing and intensity of the renewal is crucial. Consider the act of brushing our teeth. We brush our teeth, right? Every day, right? We don't say, "Oh, I'll brush them for a whole hour on Saturday; that should take care of it, right?" Wrong. That's not what we do. Rather than brushing intensely in spurts, we brush often and for less time. How often and how intensely depends on a lot of factors—

whether we eat gummi bears or clear soup, whether we're at home or out of the house, whether we brushed an hour ago or yesterday. Because we eat, we brush our teeth. And because we brush we'll continue to have teeth that make eating easier.

So it is with organizing. Because we take in stuff, we have to renew it appropriately. Whatever comes in—be it physical objects, information on paper or electronically mediated, clothing, gadgets, and the like—needs to be dealt with: processed, cleaned, stored, filed, or moved along. Some systems have much more to deal with than others. Some systems require more frequent attention than others. We need to refresh our systems in a manner that's timely and appropriate. If we don't, stuff clogs up the works and becomes a backlog.

Gather Data

We call on our observer to gather data about our current ways of sustaining—not only what tasks we are doing now but also how much time we spend on them and how often we do them. We establish a benchmark, a point from which to assess and adjust our maintenance habits. As in any change process, we make changes from where we are, rather than where we would like to be. Our slightly detached observer is our best ally in this delicate process. The practice sheet gives space to note our rhythm for each maintenance task.

Exactly Enough, Not Too Much

Most of us feel that we don't do enough maintenance and fear that if we got around to it at all, we would get too involved in it. The key is to find that middle ground where we do exactly enough maintenance. Enough to feel supported and comfortable. Enough to prevent a backlog. But not so much that we feel burdened.

The negative feelings around maintenance make it difficult to find that middle ground. We'd rather not even think about what, exactly, we are to do. We're ashamed that we don't do maintenance enough. We resist getting good tools or making the ones we have really support us. Consequently, we rarely file our papers. We don't make the decisions. We don't sort the mail. Clumps, clots, and piles attest to that.

Reality Check

Often we have an unrealistic sense of how much maintenance would be enough. For example, we want to do filing more often. We observe that presently we file half-heartedly once a month for as long as we can stand it, which is maybe a half hour. We think, "I should be doing this every day." But consider how unrealistic that expectation is. We're currently doing it once a month, and we expect ourselves to do it every day. Not only is that a tall order, it may also be inappropriate.

The goal is to spend exactly enough time—not too little and not too much. Better that we take just one step up in our filing rhythm, say twice a month. Each session is shorter and less exhausting; the pile is not so overwhelming. This may be perfectly sufficient. However, if it's still not enough, rather than trying to do it every day, once a week may work. We find our rhythm by gradually adjusting our frequency and intensity and then calling on our observer for feedback.

A clock and notes on our calendar help keep track of what we actually do. I remember hearing myself say, "I can't wash the kitchen floor this weekend; my Saturday morning isn't free." Then I clocked how long it actually took. From the time the bucket came out from under the sink to the time it went back was twenty minutes! And here I was saying I needed a whole morning to wash the floor. This little experiment told me that it wasn't as much a question of time as of inclination. When we get good data on how long tasks actually take, we may be pleasantly surprised. Alternatively, our estimates may be too meager. We need to acknowledge the actual time and effort involved so that we don't get discouraged. A reality check gets expectations in line with what actually happens.

How to Do It—Good Tools Used Well

Maintenance without good tools is a struggle. With them, it can be easy and inviting, even a joy. In the example of brushing our teeth, we have the brush, paste, glass, and floss, all arranged right there in the bathroom where we use them. So it is with organizing. For sorting mail, we need appropriate "acceptor sites" for the "fallout" from the sort. For filing papers, we need accessible, well-set-up files that aren't too stuffed. For scheduling events, we need an inviting calendar in which to list them. For maintenance reading, we need a comfortable spot to settle down in. Beautiful, useful, well-placed tools make Sustaining possible, and even enjoyable. We can look to the chapters on Staging, Storing, and Imagining to identify good tools. *(See pages 85, 97, and 131, respectively.)*

It may take a while to learn to use the tools. Remember how awkward flossing was the first time? So with organizing. If we've never had well-set-up files before, we can expect to take a while getting used to them. Using new sustaining tools can be awkward at first, but with conscious attention, we can use them ever more gracefully.

Sustaining While Addressing a Backlog

If we have a lot of stuff backed up from all the times we didn't maintain our systems, there's often an urge to say, "I'll take care of the backlog first; then I'll deal with the stuff coming in." What is that but an invitation to create another backlog? With Threshold Skills to help get into and back out of organizing, we can chip away at the backlog bit by bit. At the same time, Sustaining keeps incoming stuff moving through the system. It's best to do both practices in tandem. Just as some mouths require orthodontia, some organizing situations ask for drastic, transformative measures, yet we don't stop brushing our teeth just because we have braces.

See Beginning, page 53 and Ending, page 41

A big backlog may be a sign that there's too much coming in. This, we remember, is indeed within our control. If we bring it in, we will, someday and in some way, have to deal with it. Shedding can firm up the "entrance requirements" into our system so that any backlog we might incur is manageable, at least from this moment on.

See Shedding, page 111

RESISTANCE TO SUSTAINING

The necessary consequence of taking anything in is having to deal with it. Since we take in stuff all the time, we have to deal with it all the time. This "staying organized" part is where we acknowledge the consequences of what we do, and it's where many of us struggle.

The Ecology of Sustaining

For most of American history, the experience was that if we felt cramped, we could always move on—there was plenty of space. Like at the Mad Hatter's tea party in *Alice in Wonderland*, if we dirtied our place at the table, we moved down to the next one. We need not clean up after ourselves; we could just leave it behind. People living on islands or in small countries don't have such luxury of space. They know, instinctively, that if they take it in, they've got to deal with it; if they dirty it, they have to clean it. At this point in time, our experience is shifting. We are beginning to acknowledge that there is no "Away" to throw something when we want to throw it away; that there is no place "Over There" that we can move on to when "Here" is dirtied or cramped. We need to deal with our stuff, here and now.

A Helpful Attitude

Although few people are thrilled to be brushing their teeth, they do it anyway and with a neutral attitude. They don't lament, "Alas, the bicuspid! I have to brush it again? Woe is me," or get heated up, "This damn canine sticks out. I'm not going to brush it!" or blame themselves, "If only I were smarter or faster or kinder or better, maybe I wouldn't be punished with having to brush these horrible teeth, day in, day out. It's a living hell!"

Sustaining, like toothbrushing, can be emotionally neutral. We identify what we have to do, we have the tools, we make the minimal commitment, and we do it. Just do it. Such tasks that our human condition requires of us can be done in many ways. We can give them kindly, appropriate attention, or be disgusted, frustrated, irritated, or embarrassed by them. The choice is ours.

Consider the tasks raising children present. We are not embarrassed that the baby needs changing; we just change it. We are not disgusted, although that may take some learning. We do not resent the child for its necessary bodily functions. We accept the whole package—the diapers along with the child.

The Gifts of Sustaining

Sustaining, the charwoman of the skills, comes bearing valuable gifts that we would be wise to respect and honor. Here are some of them.

Power: There's an exhilaration that comes when we've set up a workable sustaining system and hit our proper rhythm. Suddenly we can now operate at full power, and how satisfying that is! Every time we discharge our obligations, we feel rejuvenated and relieved, our burdens lifted. We feel renewed and refreshed, like we've just emerged from a dip in the ocean.

Wholeness: When we attend to maintaining our systems, we are fully engaged with life as a whole package, both its joys and its trials. We embrace what's dull and unpleasant as well as what's creative and spontaneous.

Fidelity: When we do Sustaining in some way or another, every day, rain or shine, happy or sad, it becomes our faithful companion. Sometimes when life is bleakest, the most healing thing we might do is sort mail or file papers.

Art: Sustaining can be done with consummate technique, art, and awareness. We can transform this "garbage work" by using beautiful, useful tools in an appropriate, satisfying rhythm. Any practice we honor with technique and beauty becomes art.

Compassion: Sustaining gives us the opportunity to move through difficult emotions like resentment, irritation, and frustration. Rather than whipping ourselves into Sustaining by force of will, we merely, simply, sustain. We step back from our distress, learn how to soothe ourselves, and call forth our kindliness and care. Sustaining binds us to our fellows and reminds us of our condition. Yes, we are human, and yes, we have to do this. We sustain, however, with compassion and forbearance rather than distaste or harshness. Through Sustaining we find connection with others and the entire procession of life.

Regular Maintenance

The trick in Sustaining your organizing systems is to spend as much time as you need, but no more. Observe how long/how often you do maintenance tasks. If you spend too much time, propose a step down, making sure your physical support systems are in place. If you spend too little time, step up the frequency and/or time spent by just a little to achieve optimum *minimal* maintenance.

Maintenance Tasks
(add your own as needed)

How Long, How Often
(note actual, propose optimum)

Sorting mail/in box _____

Reading memos, correspondence, email _____

Reading professional journals, etc. _____

Responding to communications _____

Passing it on _____

Processing bills, paper, reports, etc. _____

Copying _____

Filing _____

Calendar, scheduling, to-do planning _____

Deciding _____

Throwing away _____

Revisit Later/Much Later piles _____

_____

_____

_____

Work in Progress and Tasks As Needed

Observe how often you attend to works in progress and tasks done on an "as-needed" basis. You may need to recall the last time you did these tasks. Some tasks, like delegating, deciding, or throwing away, might be part of your regular maintenance work rather than tasks you do only on occasion as the need arises.

If you don't do these tasks often enough, increase the frequency by one step. For example, if you make new files once a year, you might try assessing if you need new files in the fall and in the spring. That may be sufficient. The goal is to do the tasks exactly enough and not too much.

Be sure to have adequate staging areas for tasks that accumulate over time. Unless you add to the material often, stage the stuff away from the most active area—the high-rent district.

Maintenance Tasks
(add your own as needed)

How Long, How Often
(note actual, propose optimum)

Project review/setup _____

Delegating _____

Deciding _____

Archiving _____

Making new files _____

Getting supplies and tools _____

Throwing away _____

_____

_____

_____

Less Frequent Tasks

These are major tasks that you do infrequently. They involve rethinking and reorienting how you live your life. Be ready, when you tackle these tasks, for some "stirring up of the dregs." Many people do these tasks once a year, say, at year-end, during "spring cleaning," or while on retreat.

Preparation and good Ending Skills make these major changes go smoothly. Be sure to allow yourself good tools, sufficient time, and an opportunity to close down the work thoroughly.

Maintenance Tasks (add your own as needed)	**How Long, How Often** (note actual, propose optimum)

Major purging _____

Setting up/revamping systems
(address book, files, etc.) _____

Major archiving _____

Life planning/major decision making _____

_____

_____

_____

_____

_____

_____

_____

_____

Everyday Engaging

We use Engaging when we

     choose clothing colors that complement our skin tone

     notice the health of plants while watering them

     participate in a support group

     clean up the yard on neighborhood cleanup day

     stop smoking on National Smoke-Out Day

Spiritual Engaging

We use Engaging when we

     recognize the patterns of what we do in Nature's workings

     acknowledge interconnections between ourselves and others, human or nonhuman

     respond to "the signs"

     act on what dreams tell us

14. Engaging
Making Connections

THROUGH GETTING ORGANIZED, we can consciously engage with life on all levels—the personal, social, and transpersonal. Our stuff engages our entire personal life—emotions, thoughts, imagination, bodily sensations, spiritual aspirations, and intuitions. Our organized, sustainable way of being in the world supports engagement with our family and friends, community and culture. On the widest-ranging level, when our organization mirrors the processes of Nature, we engage with the powers that flow through the universe.

ON THE PERSONAL LEVEL

Organizing brings our internal world of thoughts, intuitions, desires, and emotions into alignment with our external world of stuff, space, and body as we arrange stuff according to how we think, feel, and operate. With the inner personal environment in relationship with the outer physical environment, a channel opens through which not only can we exercise influence but also be influenced. Intimate engagement with our stuff may call into question our habitual use of time, energy, and attention. It may uncover a deep longing we never knew we had. It may bring us face-to-face with soul issues of holding on and letting go. It may show us our own will. The changes we make are not just on the surface but in the deep structures as well. Stuff becomes not just a problem to solve but an instrument for living deeply, meaningfully, and powerfully.

ORGANIZING IN THE WORLD

At first glance, organizing appears to be purely personal work. After all, it's our stuff and we have to deal with it. Of course, this is true. However, organizing can touch much more than the personal. It can engage us with others and help us all live authentically and sustainably. We demonstrate to others that it's possible to get organized, even in our materialistic, time-impoverished culture. By engaging with others about organizing, we spread hope and self-empowerment rather than despair and victimization. Our organizing can, in fact, influence the culture and empower us all.

Isolation

People are relieved to know that they're not alone in their disorganization. In a culture that isolates us one from the other, we think we're the only one who struggles so hard. We hide our disorganization from others. We don't talk about it. We don't invite people to dinner because of the mess on the dining room table; we make excuses whenever anyone steps into our office; we hope no one opens the closet door.

We feel ashamed, lazy, stupid, or spineless. However, this isn't so. We are in fact well-intentioned, intelligent, energetic people trying to deal with an overwhelming volume of stuff. When we acknowledge the legitimate struggles we face, we see that, indeed, we are not alone. Certainly we need to change our ways—that will take some real work—but the situation is much more complex and less personal than our isolation leads us to believe.

Organizing with Others

Once we realize we're not alone, we can come together for mutual aid. We can work hands-on with an organizing buddy, swapping time to create staging areas, helping each other rearrange space, or setting up a filing system. We can be silent witnesses for each other during sorting to help us keep to the task. We can do group brainstorms. When we hit snags, we can offer each other sympathetic support. In company with others we can let our legitimate frustrations arise, acknowledge them, and then move on.

See
Shedding,
page 111

We may find tasks to delegate. We give tasks to those talented in doing them and leave the ones only we can do to ourselves. For example, with clear shedding criteria, someone else can do the work—a housecleaner, a young person who needs extra money, or a friend with whom we can exchange services. If we lay out the task clearly, provide sufficient feedback, and monitor the work, we can settle down any anxiety that arises. Delegating fosters healthy interdependence.

Awake to the Distress

When we engage with others about organizing, all we might encounter is com-
miseration—everyone lamenting about their own disorganization. This may make
us feel less isolated, but it probably won't move us to action. Yes, many of us are
disorganized; and yes, the surrounding culture disposes us to be so. But we'd best
not stop there.

If we are to do something about our distress we need to stay awake to it. Rather
than being lulled to sleep in the bosom of a dysfunctional culture, we can wake up
to what's happening and, in solidarity with our fellows, do something different.
We can create pockets of awareness, share insights and techniques, gather support, imagine alternatives, and mobilize the collective will to take action. Although
we might not stop the onrush of information and stuff, we may change how we
deal with it. By helping our fellows stay awake and by waking others up we may
actually change the culture.

ENGAGING THE MORE-THAN-HUMAN WORLD

Not only do we have connection with our fellows through organizing, we can also
experience connection with the more-than-human world—with Nature as a whole.
The open channel between our inner and outer environments gives us a means to
invite these experiences in.

As it turns out, we're already connected to the power of Nature through every
paper on our desk. Our stuff is but one manifestation of how Nature is, in line
with the Hermetic doctrine "as above, so below." The power of Nature is like
that of water in a river. With just enough structure, as when the stream flows
through a millrace, the flow can generate power. If, however, the water flows
into porous, spongy ground, it just seeps away. Or if the stream is clogged, the
water backs up.

We can mirror Nature's ways by containing our energy with just enough structure but not too much. For example, when we clearly define categories of things
to do in our inbox, we can get a handhold on what we need to do, and thus do it
more easily. When we set up a file that reflects how we think and act, we make it
easy to locate information and use it as we choose. Organizing sets up a channel
through which our power can flow. By operating as Nature operates, right here,
right now, we can become truly effective.

LIVING THE QUESTIONS OPENS US
TO MEANING AND POWER

When we stand in the dilemma of too much stuff, too little time, and too little space, we are in that fertile place where life is richest and most real. Needleman talks about these difficult experiences as soul food "provided by God directly . . . in the form of actual . . . experiences in man's personal and collective history [which are] intended to bring comprehension to man, an understanding heart, a conscious life." At this point in our collective history, getting organized can be "the means by which to experience life with ever-increasing consciousness."[12]

Needleman says, "Man provides freedom of will—conscious man's capacity to experience the contradictory forces of universal creation and, from himself, to open himself to the ultimate reconciling force."[13] When we soulfully organize, we stand in the dilemma, live the questions ever more deeply, and partake of nourishing soul food.

Engaging gives a sense of the unfathomable depths of our particular existence. We learn who "I am" in all our richness and complexity. We encounter ourselves in toto—from our petty irritations with time and space to the most fundamental structures on which our lives are built. Difficulties yield valuable, welcome lessons. Triumphs yield satisfaction and a sense of power. As we engage more fully, we encounter the Divine in our stuff—heaven in a grain of sand.

Engaging shows us that life is art, even magic. We observe our habits and our stuff as an artist contemplates the medium and the subject. We intervene in our environment as s/he shapes the clay. At times this seems like serious work, but at other times, it's play—arranging, trying out ideas, seeing how they work, adjusting, and trying something else. When we're fully engaged, a flexible responsiveness arises. We let the material speak to us. Thomas Moore in *Re-Enchantment of Everyday Life* talks of "the effectiveness that comes from being attuned to the world around us."[14] As we shape and form our environment, we give it meaning. As we align with how Nature works, we become effective, as a natural magician is effective. We live a life of meaning and power, of art and magic.

Engaging on the Personal Level

Engaging on the personal level shows how organizing work makes the connection between our physical environment and stuff, and our inner thoughts, desires, and way of being in the world. You've used Engaging all along in other practice sheets. Use this sheet to list the connections you've made between your inmost self and your stuff.

Example:

When I do (organizing activity)	What is the connection between the outer environment and my inner being?
Sorting	my "To Do" category shows how important interpersonal relationships are to me—I have a lot of phone calls/emails that represent special connections. I need to make a staging area for "contacts" that honors the importance of relationships.

When I do (organizing activity)	What is the connection between the outer environmentand my inner being?

Engaging on a Social Level

We can learn about organizing and support each other in our efforts through a self-run study group. We use the circle as the model—we all have something to learn, and we all have something to teach.

Here is a sample format for a group of four to twelve people. There is a mix of structured and unstructured time so the meeting is both productive and open to whatever comes up.

STUDY GROUP FORMAT

Beginning

Check-In.

Each person:

1. Names his/her present experience so s/he can "park" it and thus enter the circle clearly and cleanly

2. Brings up any "homework" from the last session

3. Names whatever hopes s/he has for the current session, in a brief one-to-two-minute check-in

Check-in can be timed by having a watch circulate "behind" the person speaking: the last speaker keeps time for the next one; the timekeeper hands the watch to the speaker as a signal that the time is up.

Agenda Building.
The topic for the session can:

1. Arise out of issues raised at check-in

2. Be agreed upon at the previous session, or

3. Be presented by a group member

Be sure to include times for each topic.

Open Space
The floor is then open for discussion of the topic in whatever way seems appropriate—listening-circle style, and where each person speaks in turn around the circle; free discussion; question and answer style; or another format.

Ending
The three stages of Ending can close down the study group session.

1. Name the main points that have been raised (immediate past)

2. Identify the topic and the logistical details (where, when) for next time (future)

3. Have a check-out round where each person names his/her present experience (present)

Responsibility for one's own experience is the key to a "leaderless" group. If the discussion is going far afield, anyone can speak up to refocus the group. Similarly, if someone hasn't spoken, or one person dominates the discussion, anyone can bring that fact to the group's attention.

Engaging on the Transpersonal Level

Engaging on the transpersonal level shows how organizing makes the connection between our way of being in the world and the workings of Nature. You've practiced this level of Engaging all along in other practice sheets. Use this sheet to list the connections you've made between your way of being and the grand patterns.

Example:

When I do (organizing activity)	What is the connection between what I do and how Nature works?
Shedding	In the autumn, when leaves fall, some hang on throughout the winter until just before the new leaves start emerging in the spring. I let some of my stuff go easily; other stuff I hold on to until the very last minute.

When I do (organizing activity)	What is the connection between what I do and how Nature works?

Postlude
Trusting and Tending

We've all had a crisis of faith in our organizing work. Say we set up a new filing system that works wonderfully. We're quite proud of it and use it faithfully for a time. Then "life" intervenes and the filing piles up again. We feel ourselves back at square one, no better than when we started. But are we really?

The fact is, we've had an experience that propelled us far out to our leading edge. In that experience is both our anguish and our hope. Because we know how wonderful it felt, the pain of slipping away from being organized is particularly sharp. Nonetheless, what happened can never be erased. Although we appear to backslide, our positive experience with the filing system pulls us along. We never quite revert to the old behavior. Our center shifts. New tracks are laid down. We've taken two steps forward and only one step back.

The Wheel Turns

If we expect progress to be swift, on target, and done once and for all, we're in for trouble. The fact is, progress is rarely direct. The path loops back on itself, traverses rocky boulder fields, or disappears in the fog. Despite our best intentions, strongest desires, and expert skills, we don't always do what we would like to do. Can we bear that—not with despair, cynicism, or resignation, but with grace, puzzlement, and even humor? We will not remain fully present. As Needleman says, "We will sleep, it is in our nature."[15]

Our only certainty is that the wheel will turn. If we sleep now, we will rouse later. If we are discouraged now, we will have faith later. If we are in the slough now, we will walk the crest of the hill later. We embrace our *both/and* nature as the perennial beginner who makes mistakes and the ever more able adept. We trust that when the fog clears we will indeed be on track, and so keep tending to the practice.

Back to the Source

The crisis of faith sends us back to the source, whatever that source is for us. We may revisit certain catchphrases that have given us a handle by which to grab hold of organizing. Say, we recall *Like-with-Like* and do no more than put similar things together. Or we rearrange our desktop in line with *Active/Archive*. We use *Move It On* or *End with Grace*. Doing such simple yet fundamentally important tasks renews our faith in our ability. It refreshes like spring rain.

We may remind ourselves of the connection between soulful organizing and the processes of Nature—separating and gathering, processing things and letting them go, or honoring boundaries. We become buoyed up in the stream of life again and are carried along.

We may also go back to the source by resting. Simply resting. Not recalling anything, doing anything, or even thinking about anything. We return to the matrix from which all things come and trust that what we need to continue will be given to us.

If we go back to the source, it will give us a message, perhaps not in the form, at the time, or with the information we had expected, but it comes nonetheless. Here is an example of how the messages can present themselves.

One summer day I was scouting around a pond for elderflowers. I moved slowly, all senses alert. No elder. Then I experienced an urge to veer off on a side path and found elder, in full bloom—more than I could possibly use. Had my mind been preoccupied, had I moved faster, had I not paid attention to when my feet said, "This way!" I'm sure I wouldn't have found what I did. A few days after that incident I lost my glasses near the walkways of the park I frequent. I asked for a message. Nothing came. Instead, I got new glasses with a new prescription, which was probably what I needed more than finding the old glasses.

The powers of the universe will come to our aid. Our job is to open ourselves to the messages, recognize them when they come, and gratefully acknowledge whatever gifts we receive. Thus, we develop a relationship with the larger pattern and trust in its ability to make itself known to us. We come to sense we're on the right track. With meaningful messages and the power of the larger pattern backing us up, we can then go forth, desire rekindled, intention clarified, and commitment renewed.

Making the Unmanifest Manifest

Throughout this book we've seen organizing as a creative act—calling forth categories; shaping a workable desktop, consolidating and refining stuff. Getting organized is comparable to making work for a one-artist show. It asks for sustained effort. It enfolds our whole being—our fear and anxiety, triumph and frustration, hope and despair—working with the humblest of materials. This creative act of intervening in our environment makes our thought patterns and ways of being manifest in our stuff. That harmonious connection between ourselves and our stuff opens a channel through which the powers of the universe can flow. By soulfully, creatively organizing, we become an utterly unique conduit for the grand processes and forces on which our lives depend.

Now What?

So, here we are at the end of the book, and, as with any ending, the three stages of close-down are before us—looking back to the past, ahead to the future, and here right to the present. Looking back we see the particular path that has brought us to this point. You may have worked with some practice sheets, made changes in your space, sorted papers, clothes, or books, gotten rid of stuff you no longer need. Or, you may have arrived here first, just to see what the end would be like. Regardless of your path, here you are, with a book called *The Spirit of Getting Organized* in your hands. That in itself is significant. You know that organizing is much more than making categories and setting up files. This is the moment to acknowledge that.

Looking ahead to the future, we wonder what it holds, what our soul has in store for us. As we get organized, we can more easily realize our soul's agenda. We are free to lend ourselves to an enterprise far grander than we could ever have imagined had we been caught up in disorganization distress. Our future unfolds before us, the way cleared.

As for the present, what now? We tend to organizing as we tend a garden, preparing the ground, planting the seeds, watering and weeding, using our skills. For the moment, however, it might be time to simply close down this piece of work. There are times to actively tend the garden and times to let it grow. We set aside thoughts about organizing and trust that, in good time, we will tend some more. Then we go forth and do what our soul asks of us, which is, whether we know it or not, what we've been hoping to do all along.

Catchphrases

CATCHPHRASES encapsulate the basic principles of getting organized. They give you an image to hold on to that occupies your verbal mind while your outer practice shifts.

2 Steps Forward/ 1 Step Back	Whenever we change, we need to integrate that change. If we feel we're "backsliding" we're probably really integrating—taking time to make the change our own. Even though it doesn't feel like we're "doing it," we probably are!
80/20 Rule	In any collection of items, 80 percent of the significance resides in 20 percent of the items. For example, on a to-do list of ten items, only two are really important; in a pile of magazines, only 20 percent of the words hold 80 percent of what we want out of them. Stay with the core of the material, don't get stuck in the periphery.
Active/Archive	Have things you use often close at hand, less often farther away. Put things rarely used out of sight, even out of the room (make a key to your archive if you're worried you'll forget what's there).
Eagle View/Ant View	The ant on the ground can't easily see the overall plan; the eagle in the air, can't do the actual work. Alternate between these views for optimum engagement and efficiency. Especially useful when settling down the work near the end of a session.

End with Grace	People often don't start organizing because they fear that if they start they'll never stop. Before you start, figure out how you'll stop. Choose how long to work, then set a timer a quarter to one-third of the total time before the end to settle down the work. Identify the bridging step to the next work session, put away the "fallout," acknowledge progress.
Follow the Deeper Rhythm	Underneath the fast pace of life there is a slower rhythm of the more important events that form the underpinnings of your life. When you pay attention to the deeper level, things slow down dramatically and make much more sense.
Foreground/Background	Lack of shape or depth makes your stuff (and your life) feel like undifferentiated chaos. At a distance, the *Wall Street Journal* looks gray, undifferentiated, all the same; by contrast, *USA Today* uses color and typefaces to define different stories. When your stuff feels undifferentiated and everything seems equally important, give the stuff some depth. Pull into the foreground what's important and let the rest stay in the background.
From This Moment On	You probably don't have to organize all the old stuff that's been hanging around forever. Instead, decide that from this moment on, you'll deal with things as they come in, rather than let them build up. Make a clean break. Start fresh.
Here and Now	When sorting papers, stay in the here and now—the realm of the immediate present and gross distinctions. Associating to other times/other places, decision making, creativity, etc., takes you off the task. Use gross categories and an "I Don't Know" category to prevent slipping into associations.

Holographic Organization	Each area of organization is connected to every other area, so organization efforts in one area ripple through to other areas. Head off discouragement when the job seems overwhelming by remembering that untangling just one strand helps untangle the whole. The work you accomplish in the small affects what happens in the large.
Like-with-Like	Put like things together, all the car things, all the financial things, all the rubber bands, all the unread magazines, etc. Keep *Active/Archive* in mind as well. You may end up with two places for similar material, one active and one archive.
Macro/Micro	About 80 percent of your total categories are represented in any random sample of your stuff. Whatever you learn from the sample you can apply to the entire situation.
Middle Ground	Most work happens in the middle ground between the inbox and the storage file. Honor how things actually happen by giving tools and space to the middle ground. The middle ground concept also applies to how you maintain your systems. All-or-nothing organizing takes a heavy toll—you're highly organized only a small percentage of the time; most of the time you struggle. Developing a middle ground between "all" and "nothing" allows you to be organized enough to work effectively most of the time.
Move It On	Move things in the direction they're headed: put things to pass on near the door, things to go upstairs on the steps, things to file on top of the file cabinet. Do this rather than jumping up to put each item away as it appears.

Opportunity Cost

"The true cost of something is what you have to give up in order to get it." This economics principle helps identify what you have to say no to in order to say yes to constructive change. Think of all the things you might have to give up in order to be organized—the all-purpose excuse, your image of yourself as a creative (read messy) person, your convenient hiding behind a sea of paper. Then make peace with what you'll have to say no to. This clears the way for change to take hold.

Plate of Spaghetti

With a big backlog it's easy to get overwhelmed and discouraged. Think of a big plate of spaghetti: you eat and eat and it doesn't seem like you're making any progress; then gradually you begin to notice that there's more plate than spaghetti. Stay with it until you begin to notice change.

Prime Real Estate

Wherever you can reach as you work is prime real estate—the high-rent district. Make sure that everything within that area supports your work—things used frequently, tools to "park" current work, holders to collect stuff moving to other areas. Clear away anything finished, broken, or extra to a more appropriate location.

Reality Check

Use a timer to see how long tasks really take. When they take too long, be sure your support systems are in place.

Rope It Off

When doing large, multisession organizing jobs, put up a strong "police line" around the work so you don't get overwhelmed or distracted by the tasks you've decided not to do now.

Start Small

Major changes come from small steps taken consciously and carefully cultivated. The little seed of organization will grow and and take hold with conscious attention.

Strengths<=> Weaknesses	Every preference is both a strength and a weakness. We don't have to get rid of anything or become someone else to be organized. We just have to use what we have appropriately and develop a range of skills. For example, a penchant for being distracted is a strength when many things require our attention but a weakness when we need to focus. Developing alternative skills and entertaining alternative possibilities lets us choose the technique to match the job.

Basic Assumptions
That Inform This Work

THE METAPHORS, analogies, and stories in this book come from the practices I have pursued over relatively long periods of time. They form my thoughts and feelings, beliefs and body. Through them I seek to align with Nature and the Divine, a pursuit I've followed for as long as I can remember. As a little child I was a fervent churchgoer; as an adolescent I practiced Zen; over the past twenty-five years I've practiced an earth-centered spirituality.

My current practices are dowsing, dreamwork, using the body as teacher, astrology, and artistic pursuits—classical and improvisational music, dance, and storytelling, all as an amateur. Each practice informs the others, resulting in herbal medicine, wild food gathering, and dancing in the woods. I've been influenced by what I've read as well as what I've practiced. The basic assumptions on which this book rests have evolved through the years. I list them here.

ALL THINGS ARE ONE

Many earth-centered spiritual practices, as well as many "book religions" take as a basic premise that everything is connected. Each being is linked through a matrix to all beings. What an individual does affects the whole system. Gaia consciousness goes even further to say that all beings of the earth are organs of the larger planet organism. Humans are the organs of the Earth responsible for aesthetic appreciation, just as wings are the organs of the bird responsible for flying.

A corollary of this belief is that I have a part in and am, in a very real way, responsible for, everything that happens. I can exercise influence, even shape the course of events. In turn, I am influenced by what happens here, or anywhere, in the universe. For example, I may feel my boss pressuring me to work overtime. I'm irritated by his demands and wish he would stop. On another level, these emotions are indicators of an atmosphere of pressure to which we both, and the surrounding culture, are contributing. Thinking in this way, there is much I can do to make a shift, and in fact, change the world. If it's merely a question of his demand versus my desire, an opportunity to influence on another level has been missed.

A second corollary is that all beings and processes are of value. Some years ago there was a minor bloom of mosquito-borne encephalitis in our area. Although there were certainly no fatalities and hardly any illness, people rushed to wage war on the insects. The assumption was that people were more important than animals. I do not subscribe to that view. All species and beings have value; none intrinsically more than another. Whatsoever you do to the least of my creatures/brethren, this you do unto me.

A third corollary is that what works in the small works in the large. What we learn here applies there as well. When we learn how to handle the stuff on our desk we're learning how to handle the universe. Nothing is wasted; everything is useful.

THE UNIVERSE IS GOOD

In Taoism, some forms of Buddhism, and various forms of earth spirituality, the universe is imbued with basic goodness. The universe works, and that is good. There is no need to fix or fiddle. Things have been good, are good, and will be good. It just may not look like that from our point of view.

There's a traditional Chinese tale that illustrates the point. A farmer's horse ran off. His neighbor laments, "What bad luck!" The farmer says, "Maybe good, maybe bad—we'll see." Later that day the horse returns with a beautiful wild mare accompanying it. "Oh," exclaims the neighbor, "What good luck!" The farmer says, "Maybe good, maybe bad—we'll see." In the process of taming the mare, the farmer's son falls off and breaks his leg. "What bad luck," says the neighbor. And, of course, the farmer says, "Maybe good, maybe bad—we'll see." The next week sergeants come to town to draft all able-bodied young men, and the farmer's son is spared. So, what's good, what's bad? When we step back from our nearsighted view, we might be able to see.

The assumption that the universe is good is a major sticking point with "book religions" like Christianity, Judaism, Islam, Buddhism, and Hinduism. These religions say that there's something wrong, bad, or tainted—in us, in the creation— that needs to be changed, saved, or redeemed. When I finally made contact with religions and spiritualities that work on other models I felt a deep sense of relief and homecoming. My experience with the outdoors and how things work never really supported the salvationist point of view. Although I'm not 100 percent comfortable saying "the universe is good," having experienced some pretty nasty stuff floating around out there, generally, it's what I believe.

My Soul Has an Agenda

The soul is engaged in its own evolution, which it accomplishes through taking on an earthly body and putting itself in the best possible circumstances to learn a particular lesson. Each lifetime has an agenda—the lesson to be learned this time around. In some systems, this is the daimon—the force that drives the life. The soul's (or daimon's) agenda may have little regard for its human's comfort. All it wants is to learn.

I can discover this agenda. I can pray, observe my desires, longings, and inclinations. I can use techniques like dowsing, I Ching, tarot, or contacting spirit guides. Over a span of years, I begin to see the shape that my life is taking, and from those observations, deduce the agenda. Can I know, reliably, clearly, and in detail what the daimon, or the gods, or the soul has in store? I doubt it. False prophets rely on what they think is divine instruction. We (or they) find, in the end, that the instructions were but personal inventions. Discernment is tricky.

I Can Exercise Will

I can choose, with full responsibility, to follow the soul's agenda or not. At every moment, in every circumstance, I can choose what to think about, what action to take, where to direct my energy and attention. I can freely follow my life's purpose, and consciously align myself with the agenda I have discerned . . . or not. The agenda smacks of fate, yet the choice suggests free will. Dancing at the midpoint between these poles is what's needed.

I believe that the beyond-human powers are less interested in us bowing down to them than in our working with them. They invite partnership and cocreativity if we are but respectful and discerning. When my will aligns with theirs, I am doing what I am meant to do.

Awareness Helps, Usually

In this free will/agenda enterprise, consciousness helps. As I look back on my life, I see so many moments where awareness was my greatest strength. If I had shut my eyes, things might have gone much differently. Or they may have worked out exactly the same in the end, but at a great price. I often prefer knowing over not knowing.

Yet, I am all too ready to stay in the dark and discount messages from my daimon. I safely pretend that I don't have a clue as to what it's all about, when in fact, I do. In the Steve Martin movie, *The Man with Two Brains*, Martin, the mad scientist, stands before the portrait of his dead wife to ask for guidance. He implores, "Give me a sign. Give me a sign!" The painting spins around, releases bursts of light, and makes a whirring sound. Then we see Martin, still standing in front of the spinning portrait, repeating, "Give me a sign. Give me a sign." So often, the signs are there and we see them, but we don't believe what we see.

Resources

SOURCES THAT INFLUENCED THIS BOOK

Abram, David. *The Spell of the Sensuous: Perception and Language in a More-Than-Human World*. New York: Pantheon Books, 1996.

Batstone, Philip. Personal conversations 1970–1976.

Deikman, Arthur J. *The Observing Self: Mysticism and Psychotherapy*. Boston: Beacon Press, 1982.

Dillard, Annie. *Pilgrim at Tinker Creek*. New York: Harper Perennial, 1974.

MacLaren, Karla. *Emotional Genius: Discovering the Deepest Language of the Soul*. Columbia, CA: Laughing Tree Press, 2001.

Moore, Thomas. *The Re-Enchantment of Everyday Life*. New York: HarperCollins, 1996.

Needleman, Jacob. *Time and the Soul*. New York: Currency/Doubleday, 1998.

Needleman, Jacob. *Money and the Meaning of Life*. New York: Currency/Doubleday, 1991, 1994.

Quinn, Daniel. *The Story of B*. New York: Bantam Books, 1996.

Rezendes, Paul. *Tracking and the Art of Seeing*. Charlotte, VT: Camden House Publishing, 1992.

Swimme, Brian. *The Universe Is a Green Dragon*. Santa Fe, NM: Bear & Co., 1984.

Weed, Susun S. *Healing Wise*. Woodstock, NY: Ash Tree Publishing, 1989.

GENERAL RESOURCES

Center for a New American Dream, 6930 Carroll Ave., Suite 900, Tacoma Park, MD 20912.

DMA Mail Preference Service, PO Box 9008, Farmingdale, NY 11735-9008; (Telephone Service, PO Box 9014, zip 11735-9014). Write here to get off lists.

New Road Map Foundation, PO Box 15981, Seattle, WA 98115.

Wurman, Richard Saul. *Information Anxiety*. New York: Doubleday, 1989.

DIVINATION RESOURCES

Arcati, Kristyna. *I Ching, a Beginner's Guide*. London: Hodder & Stoughton, 1994.

Garen, Nancy. *Tarot Made Easy*. New York: Fireside, 1989.

Meadows, Kenneth. *Rune Power*. Boston: Element, 1996.

Woods, Walt. *Letter to Robin: A Mini-Course in Pendulum Dowsing*. St. Johnsbury, VT: American Society of Dowsers, 1995.

CREATIVITY RESOURCES

Delaney, Gayle. *In Your Dreams: A New Kind of Dream Dictionary*. New York: Harper Collins, 1997.

Gawain, Shakti. *Creative Visualization*. San Rafael, CA: Whatever Publishing, 1978.

Petty, Geoffrey. *How to Be Better at Creativity*. London: Kogan Page, 1997.

Sher, Barbara. *Wishcraft*. New York: Ballantine Books, 1986.

MEDITATION RESOURCES

Chodron, Pema. *When Things Fall Apart*. Boston: Shambhala, 2000.

Kornfield, Jack. *After Ecstasy, the Laundry*. New York: Bantam, Doubleday, 2001.

Thich Nhat Hanh. *The Miracle of Mindfulness*. Boston: Beacon Press, 1996.

SECONDARY RESOURCES

Hyde, Lewis. *The Gift: Imagination and the Erotic Life of Property.* New York: Vintage Books, 1983.

Moore, Thomas. *Care of the Soul.* New York: HarperCollins, 1992.

Nicoll, Maurice. *Living Time.* London: Watkins, 1952.

Palmer, Parker J. *The Company of Strangers.* New York: The Crossroad Publishing Company, 1991.

Notes

1   Jacob Needleman, *Money and the Meaning of Life*. (New York: Currency/Doubleday, 1991, 1994), pp. 33–37.

2   Heather McHugh, unpublished poem quoted in personal conversation with Philip Batstone, 1972.

3   Needleman, p. 163.

4   Arthur J. Deikman, *The Observing Self: Mysticism and Psychotherapy*. (Boston: Beacon Press, 1982), p. 96.

5   Margaret Starbird, *Woman with the Alabaster Jar*. (Santa Fe, NM: Bear and Company, 1993), p. 176

6   Moses Maimonides, *The Guide for the Preplexed*, trans. M. Friedlaender, (New York: Dover Publications, 1956), p. 270 quoted in Needleman, p. 217–8.

7   John Kenneth Galbraith, *The Affluent Society*, 4th ed. (New York: New American Library, 1984), p. 121 ("One cannot defend production as satisfying wants if that production creates the wants.") quoted in Needleman, p. 28.

8   Needleman, pp. 53–72.

9   Thomas Moore, *The Re-Enchantment of Everyday Life*. (New York: HarperCollins, 1996), p. xiii.

10 Moore, p. xix.

11 Eccles. 3:1.

12 Needleman, p. 224.

13 Needleman, p. 224.

14 Moore, p. 373.

15 Needleman, p. 136.

Index